Transforming Body Image

Transforming Body Image

Learning to Love the Body You Have

by
Marcia Germaine
Hutchinson, Ed.D.

THE CROSSING PRESS / Freedom, California 95019

The exercises in this book are designed to elicit deep psychological material. Anyone who has a history of psychiatric disorder or emotional instability, or who is currently using major tranquilizers or anti-depressant medication is advised to consult a qualified mental health professional before doing these exercises.

Cover illustration by Carole Odell
Cover design by William Houston
Text design by Martha J. Waters and Betsy Bayley
Typesetting by Martha J. Waters
Printed in the U.S.A.

Library of Congress Cataloging-in-Publication Data

Hutchinson, Marcia Germaine.
   Transforming body image.

   1. Body image.   2. Self-acceptance.   3. Reducing--
Psychological aspects.   I. Title.
BF 697.5.B63H87   1985   158'.1   85-17524
ISBN 0-89594-173-2
ISBN 0-89594-172-4 (pbk.)

Acknowledgments

A book is the culmination of a long chain of events, and thanks are due to many people. My long-time friend, Donna Mildvan, suggested that my doctoral dissertation needed to become a book. A friend, Marilyn Taylor, led me to Kathleen Spivack, my relentlessly positive literary guide, who cheer-led me through a year of writer's anxiety, sharing the secrets of the Viennese along the way. Carole Odell, my dear friend, graced the book jacket with her intelligent, sensitive, and beautiful artwork that captures so well the essence of this material. I'd like to acknowledge Andrea Fleck Clardy. And finally, Elaine Goldman Gill, my editor, whose warmth, humanity, and profound commitment to this project came through in every red editorial squiggle.

I have drawn intellectual inspiration from Moshe Feldenkrais, Fritz Perls, Roberto Assagioli, Win Wenger, Robert Masters, and Jean Houston.

My dog, Lina, has been my faithful companion throughout. Snuggled calmingly nearby while I typed endlessly, she was a constant reminder of peace, ease, and simplicity.

Most of all I want to thank my husband, Bill Hutchinson. He held down the fort and kept the home fires burning (literally) while I was lost in thought and/or deadlines. His patience, understanding, and emotional support provided a holding environment in which I could create.

Thank you all.

Dedicated to the many women who had the courage to trust me and my method, the courage to dive into deep, unknown waters. If you saw yourselves as I see you, you would know what beauty is. Without you there would be no book.

> *In the scenery of spring*
> *there is nothing superior*
> *nothing inferior;*
> *flowering branches*
> *are by nature*
> *some short*
> *some long.*
>
> *Zen Proverb*

Contents

Introduction 11

SECTION 1: Straying From Home 19

I. Woman's Self/Woman's Body 20

II. Making Your Imagination An Ally 31

SECTION 2: Tools For Transformation 35

III. Knowing What You Want 36

    Exercise 1: Making Choices 36

IV. Training Your Imaginal Muscles 39

    Exercise 2: Learning to Relax 39

    Exercise 3: Sensory Remembering 42

    Exercise 4: The Imaginal Body 45

V. Getting To Know Your Body Image 48

    Exercise 5: Body Scanning 49

    Exercise 6: Imaginary Mind-Mirror 54

    Exercise 7: Opening Doors 57

VI. Cultural Roots 63

VII. Muckraking 67

    Exercise 8: Rolling Back the Years 68

    Exercise 9: Family Portrait 71

    Exercise 10: Parental Images 74

VIII. Who's Wrong With Your Body Image? 80

    Exercise 11: Imaginary Visitors 80

    Exercise 12: Wheel of Chains 83

IX. Holding On To What? 88

    Exercise 13: Cloaks of Identity 86

    Exercise 14: Woman in a Trap 92

X. Finding Your Voice. 97
    Exercise 15: Meet Your Saboteurs. 99
    Exercise 16: Body Talk. .104
    Exercise 17: Express Mail. 107
XI. Exercising Your Body-Mind. 109
    Exercise 18: One Pill Makes You Larger. 109
    Exercise 19: Moving Attitudes. 113
XII. Learning To Love The Body You Have. 120
    Exercise 20: Mirror Breathing. 121
    Exercise 21: Imaginal Massage. 125
XIII. Putting It All Together. 129
    Exercise 22: Transformational Body Myth. 130

    SECTION 3: The Road Home. 137
XIV. Four Women in Process. 138
    Afterword 147
    Resources 150

INTRODUCTION

My own struggle with my body stretches back into early childhood. It was clear to me that my body was not quite right: it was too large, too chunky, too muscular. It could never be sufficiently petite and delicate to be considered feminine and beautiful by the standards that prevailed during the forties and fifties when I was growing up. I have a body that is sturdy and robust even at its thinnest. It's the kind of body that exceeds the height-weight tables even when there isn't an ounce of extra fat on it. It's the kind of body whose unique proportions do not easily adapt to ready-to-wear clothing. And finally, it is the kind of body that gains weight at the sight of food and loses weight and keeps it off only with the greatest hardship and constant deprivation.

My body image, the way I see and feel about my body, has been my greatest personal stumbling block. I was obsessed with my body and its awfulness, its deviation from what was socially acceptable and from my own ideals. No area of my life escaped the ravages of my obsession. I spent most of my 43 years letting my body's imperfections taint my sense of the real person living inside. I used to look at my body and forget that inside there lived a kind, intelligent, and valuable human being—me.

I am struck and saddened by how much power I have given to others to shape my behavior and the way I have felt about myself. I had the absolute conviction that others were judging me as harshly as I judged myself, as a bundle of flaws. I was shy, awkward, and withdrawn, and this made it very easy for people to ignore or reject me. I made it happen.

In group situations I really became invisible and was ignored. This hurt me a great deal because I was aware of how many opportunities I was missing: to meet interesting people, to share my knowledge, to get recognition for my abilities and personal qualities. I spent years feeling like a nobody. No one noticed me therefore I did not exist. The worse I felt, the more effectively I hid myself away. I harbored secret feelings that I was really an undiscovered treasure and that some select people with vision would recognize me. Indeed some did, but I hate to think how many did not.

Every new encounter with a woman made me feel self-conscious, intimidated, envious, and inadequate. I used to look at women who were thin and imagine how happy they were, how they had partners who loved and admired them, how they felt easy and uninhibited every time they took off their clothes or sauntered along the beach. I no longer see physical beauty as a guarantee of happiness. I no longer delude myself that if I were thin a series of wonderful and miraculous events would take place. In fact those periods of my life when I was thin (although of course I didn't believe it at the time) were in no major ways happier than any of my fat times. It was easier to find clothes that fit me, but that was all. I never felt free of the judgment of others (because I still judged my body and myself severely). I never attracted men who were interested in me or capable of carrying on a serious relationship. I met men who were interested in me for the wrong reasons, because I looked good at their side. The truth of the matter is that those men with whom I have established lasting and meaningful relationships met and accepted me when my weight was on the high side.

My own weight has run the gamut from low to high, mostly high. My genes, my constitution, and my ethnic heritage, predispose me to overweight. And the years of chronic dieting, deprivation, and overeating have deranged my metabolic system to the extent that now, even though I am a moderate and conscious eater, it is virtually impossible for me to be anything but overweight.

There is no question that it is difficult to be a heavy woman in a thin world. It has been the source of much pain for me over the years. And it has also built character. I, like most people, had unquestioningly accepted the many stereotypes about fat people and used them as weapons to torture myself for being larger than average. Frankly, I can no longer identify the me that I know with those stereotypes. I have seen little evidence of compulsive overeating in my life for many, many years. I am emotionally healthy, in control of my life. I am healthy, strong, fit, supple, and graceful. And my life includes intimacy, friendship, meaningful work, and a life style of my own design. And I'm overweight.

After much struggle, I have grown to accept my body as it is. I have come to realize that the superhuman effort it would require for me to lose and keep off my extra weight is better applied to more important (to me) projects such as writing this book. It is a choice I make.

My years of anguish around my body image drove me to therapy, innumerable diets, dance classes, silent suffering, commiserating with other women—you name it. Still I could not unravel this stubborn knot until I stumbled on an important clue.

For several years I studied the Feldenkrais Method, an ingenious body-mind, movement-oriented therapy hoping to cure a chronic back problem. One phase of the method consists of movement sequences designed to help you learn through playful, childlike discovery how your body is designed to operate. Experiencing my body in the Feldenkrais way not only helped my back immensely—it also gave me a heightened awareness and appreciation of the intelligence and functional integrity of my body. It instilled in me an attitude of playfulness and discovery about my body as well as a new sense of ease and fluidity.

At the last meeting of our Feldenkrais study group, a video camera recorded our floor movements and, with considerable trepidation, I watched the playback on the monitor. What I saw (through the distortions of my body image) was a huge lump with enormous hindquarters. I was inconsolable.

Somehow my visual impression was translated into a kinesthetic experience. My image (the one I saw on the monitor) became a feeling. I felt my body as a tree-stump: too short, too compact, too immobile, too much. At that moment I felt an intense hatred of my body. This painful experience (both the image that I saw and the image that I felt) made me question how women get locked into distortions about their bodies and, more important, it directed me to find ways that might *alter* a woman's relationship to her body so that she could accept it.

Several things became clear. My body image had very little to do with my physical body. In fact they were quite separate. It was possible for me to look lovely from an objective point of view and yet feel fat and ugly. And the reverse was also true. Image and reality are separate and distinct phenomena when there is a distorted body image.

I realized that my body image was a special kind of *image,* a product of my imagination. I had a strong hunch that it could therefore be altered by using my imagination in a controlled and directed manner. Five years ago I used my doctoral dissertation* as an opportunity to explore the problem of body image hoping to find a creative solution.

---

* Sankowsky, M.H. (aka M. Hutchinson) "The effect of a treatment based on the use of guided visuo-kinesthetic imagery on the alteration of negative body-cathexis in women." Unpublished doctoral dissertation. Boston University, 1981.

I set up a controlled experiment using a group of women who identified themselves as having negative body images. After administer-
ing tests of body image (I asked each woman to rate her feelings
about different aspects of her body and her self) and interviewing all
the women, I randomly divided them into two comparable groups. I
guided one group through a 7-week therapeutic process that I
created, called Transforming Body Image. During the experimental
workshop these women were led through a series of exercises that
used their imagination as a way of learning about their body image
and healing its wounds. Although they went through the workshop in
a group, each woman worked independently and privately, using a
journal with guiding questions to process her experience. The other
group of women passed the seven weeks in their usual manner. After
the workshop ended I tested and interviewed all the women again. I
found that the women who had experienced the workshop were
significantly changed both in their body images and their self images.
A follow-up questionnaire six months later indicated that for most of
the women the changes were holding and even deepening.

Since those early days I have adjusted, expanded, and refined this
process in the Transforming Body Image workshop for women in the
Boston area. The workshop consists of ten weekly two-hour
meetings. In addition to the work with imagery and journal-keeping,
the workshop now includes Feldenkrais movement work. I still use a
group format in which each woman does her own inner work in the
context of a supportive group. It is this process of Transforming
Body Image that I offer you in this book.

Over the last five years I have felt a great satisfaction watching
many women grow more contented with their bodies. Many have
come to appreciate their bodies just the way they are. Others have
chosen to make loving changes and refinements in their appearance.
For some, a new compassion for their bodies has helped them to
listen to and take care of their bodies in a way that has helped normalize their weight and health.

In the years since I began work on my body image my values have
begun to move from the inside outward rather than the other way. I
have really learned to love and respect and accept myself as I am.
This has been a powerful and significant change in me. I am not going to tell you that the appearance of my body or your body is irrelevant. But I will say that unless you love and accept your *self,* unless
you *feel* beautiful *inside,* you will not see your outer beauty, let alone
believe it or enjoy it.

My own process continues. I still have bad days when I'm convinced that I'm repulsive. But most of the time I live in a state of truce—I can enjoy my body and all the ways it moves me through life. I don't delude myself into thinking that my body will be declared the new standard of beauty for the world. I don't delude myself about my body at all. I know that there is room for improvement when I'm ready, if I choose. But, more important, I know that I am much, much more than my body—my sense of my own worth is not attached to my body.

In my search for a peaceful relationship with my body I have not had the luxury of being led through one of my workshops or of being taken by the hand through a book such as this. My own peace has come from trial and error. Certainly the process of creating *Transforming Body Image* and listening to the stories of hundreds of women has deepened my understanding of what is involved in straying from and reclaiming our bodies. I have done much deep soul searching, and psychological housecleaning. I have become willing to forgive others who have hurt me and to forgive myself for not looking the way I always dreamed I should look. My work with the Feldenkrais Method has given me a feeling of ease, comfort, and grace in movement that pervades my experience of living in my body. My body feels more like a home.

Changing my body image has meant holding on to my own vision of myself even when some people sometimes reflect a different and less accepting vision back to me. Along the way I have had the help of friends who have loved me regardless of how I look. But it took a shift in my own internal perception before I could really let that in. *Feeling* lovely is more central than *looking* lovely. The inner shift precedes the outer change.

Most profound to me was my experience with the many women for whom I designed this work. Witnessing the suffering of the many truly lovely women who hate their bodies has helped me to challenge many long held assumptions about outer beauty. With each encounter my own conviction to let go of this struggle became stronger. Each interview brought home to me the futility and waste involved in hating our bodies. Throughout this book I will share with you their pains, their struggles, and their progress.

The majority of women in our culture do not accept their bodies as they are. In fact, it is a rare woman today who has a healthy body image, who is not actively doing battle with her body. Eating disorders such as anorexia nervosa, bulimia (binging-purging)—once rare and obscure conditions—have now become commonplace. They are extreme symptoms of the body/mind split so common in our culture. When the mind and body are at war, they no longer work together for the good of the whole being. The body is experienced as a foreign object or hated antagonist.

The inability to feel at home in our bodies can make life miserable on every front. We are so busy obsessing over what is wrong with us—whether it's our weight, misproportion, wrinkles, pimples, excess hair, or functional limitations—that we fail to develop our potential as human beings. If we could harness a tiny fraction of the energy and attention wasted in body hate and use it as fuel for creativity and self-development, just think how far we could travel toward our life goals.

Any movement toward self-improvement must be propelled not by disgust and self-rejection, but by a realistic acceptance of who *we already are* and a desire to be the best possible version of that reality. Any diet or regime that we impose on our bodies that is inspired by self-disgust will be punitive and our bodies will rebel and fight us at every turn. Any fitness program we undertake will make us fit only if it is done with awareness and gentleness. Only when our motives are based on love and respect, will our bodies respond as we wish them to. Only when we know and accept who we are, can we change.

The task of coming to a place of union within yourself involves a lifelong process of listening to your body, of respecting and trusting its messages. It involves letting go of the negative tapes that you chronically run in your head while at the same time giving stronger voice to the part of you that sees clearly and wants to be whole again. You will learn to accept the idiosyncracies of your own body type and to adopt realistic and gentle goals for realizing your greatest potential. It is a process not of changing your body but of changing your *outlook*.

Isn't it about time that someone told you that your body is all right, just the way it is? Isn't it about time you picked up a book that offers you a road back to mind-body wholeness instead of some new way to "fix" yourself? *Transforming Body Image* isn't about changing your body. It's about learning to love and accept the body you already have. It's about making your body a home that you can live in.

•

How To Use This Book

This is a self-help book adapted from my workshops. It is designed so that you can proceed from step to step on your own, using the tools and guidance provided. There is a natural order to the exercises. Some can stand alone, but if you follow them in the order given you will benefit the most. Each exercise is a stepping stone to the next. Simply reading through the exercises will do something for you, but for this process to transform you, you must *do* the exercises.

These exercises are self-exploratory experiences that will enlighten you about your body image—what it is, how it has come to be the way it is, what is right for your body, how to heal the wounds and shift the attitudes that keep you from perceiving your body and yourself as beautiful, healthy, and whole.

This book is not a quick fix. You did not develop your current body image overnight—nor will you transform it overnight. For some of you the road will be one mile, for others one hundred miles. Allow yourself ten weeks or even longer to work through this book, pacing yourself so that you can assimilate the changes. It takes time to integrate such an important shift in attitude toward yourself. So please respect your own timing.

It is possible to do the work alone, but if you know other women who struggle with the same issues, it will help to go through the process with them. Your body image is delicate psychological territory. Many of the exercises may evoke strong feelings, some painful. Working with others will provide support and encouragement to persevere.

The exercises in this book rely very heavily on the positive and controlled use of the imagination—that powerhouse for healing which we all possess.

The exercises are presented so that it is possible to read each step and then go inside to do the work in your imagination. You will have a deeper and more powerful experience if you let someone else lead you through the exercises. There are several ways to do this. If you are working with a friend or a small group, you can take turns leading each other through the exercises. If you are working alone, it will help to tape the exercises from the scripts provided, pausing after each step [. . .] to allow time to work with your imagery. I have also recorded the exercises in this book on a set of cassette tapes which you can order. (See the Resource Section of the book for ordering information.)

Each exercise has a brief introduction that sets the stage. In it you will often find *seed questions* that will help you to begin thinking about issues that are relevant to the exercise that follows. Please take the time to reflect on these questions as your thoughts will facilitate the imagery that follows.

Following each exercise is a *worksheet* which contains questions to help you process your imaginal experience. The best way to use the *worksheet* is to write down the answers to these questions immediately after completing the exercise. Images like dreams are very fragile, and the longer you delay at this step, the more your imaginal experience will evaporate. The *worksheet* is a very important phase of the work, so please do not skip over it. This work is designed to use both halves of your brain. The right half does the imaging, and the left half processes the imagery through language. The two together will give you a whole-brained, integrated experience.

Finally, in *Guiding Words* I have included some words of guidance as well as verbatim experiences of some of the women who have participated in my workshops. Their stories will stimulate your associations and will illustrate important points.

Section 1
Straying From Home

I

WOMAN'S SELF/
WOMAN'S BODY

*To men a man is but a mind. Who cares
What face he carries or what form he wears?
But woman's body is the woman.*

Ambrose Bierce

Your Self

As a woman your body is so intimately linked with your sense of self that your body attitudes readily spill over into self attitudes. If you are dissatisfied with your self, you will most likely take it out on your body. Similarly, if you are down on your body, you will chip away at your self-esteem. In women, body-esteem and self-esteem appear to be married to each other. (In men this is not true.) Most women who devalue their bodies also devalue themselves. Or is it that most women who dislike themselves also dislike their bodies? It is a classic chicken and egg question.

As women, we are raised to see our bodies as the means to achieving control of our lives. We often forget that we are more than our bodies. We blame and punish our bodies for our failures and disappointments — we don't look at other features of our personalities and behavior that could use overhauling. It is this maligned body and the image that we have of it that we haul around, effecting all areas of our lives.

When that attractive person failed to notice us, it must have been because we were too fat or not pretty enough. It had nothing to do with the fact that we were frozen in fear. When we were passed over for that promotion at work, our body was the culprit for its failure to achieve the right professional look. We overlooked the fact that our major competitor had been busy impressing the boss with her/his ideas while we hung back.

When we relate to another person, she or he becomes a mirror that reflects back to us our own vision of ourselves. If that vision is positive and healthy, others will see and respond to that same wholesomeness. If we experience our bodies and ourselves as negative or lacking in some way, others will experience us in that light. We are incredibly powerful in shaping others' reactions to us.

•

How do your feelings about your body affect the choices you make in social situations?

•

Many of us feel shy or awkward around people. We may hide and withdraw before others have the chance to accept or reject us. And, interestingly enough, when others do seek us out, we find reasons to reject them. Like Groucho Marx, we wouldn't want to belong to any club that would admit us as a member. Many women withdraw completely from social contact. This leads to a narrow and restricted social world which in turn breeds loneliness and a sense of inadequacy that make matters worse.

It is very difficult to relate to others when we are thoroughly absorbed in our worries and obsessions about our bodies. This kind of self-absorption can distance us from others, blocking the possibility for contact and closeness and draining our energy and interest away from relating. We miss out on opportunities for genuine human connection.

If you are like the many women I have worked with, it is likely that you automatically compare yourself to other women, especially women you meet for the first time. You wonder whether you are prettier or uglier, fatter or thinner. Women who struggle with their bodies are very severe judges of themselves and often of others. The comparison is painful and senseless, breeding envy, self-doubt, and distance. You are you and they are they. Moreover, the way that you see other women may be very different from how they feel inside. I have spent years interviewing and working with women who are objectively very lovely and attractive but who see themselves as fat, ugly, ungainly, and inadequate.

Many women with poor body images withdraw from competition with other women. Taking themselves out of the running protects them from failing. It is amazing how many women use this as a rationale for remaining overweight or for not projecting the beauty or pizazz available to them. We are afraid to incur the envy of our sisters and possibly lose their friendship. But what a price to pay!

Our negative feelings about our bodies really create difficulties in our intimate relationships with either men or women. We are brainwashed to believe that we have to be beautiful or at least thin in order to be sexual or sexually desirable. Therefore many of us deny ourselves the pleasures of love and intimacy. One woman put it succinctly, "I automatically think I'm seen as fat and therefore undesirable. How could I possibly have a relationship with a man? What man would want me?" With such strong feelings of inadequacy, the fear of rejection becomes very powerful, to be avoided at any cost. We turn down invitations, stay home and eat and feel sorry for ourselves. Some of us allow ourselves to choose only dependent partners who will not reject us because they need us too much. This type of relationship is usually doomed to failure. We avoid possible sexual experiences by not allowing ourselves to flirt or provoke interest in a potential lover. Or we adopt the role of friend to that person rather than lover. In some cases it is our own sexuality that we fear, thinking it such a powerful force that we literally run away from it.

It is almost as if we walk around with signs that say, "Make sure you notice how fat and disgusting my thighs are so you can reject me." How many of us have sabotaged our love relationships by criticizing our bodies? One woman saw how she brought it on herself.

> "I make it into a huge issue and I can't believe it isn't for my partner. He tells me he loves me and that I'm very attractive to him, but I don't believe him. He's only saying that to make me feel good or because he feels sorry for me. I mistrust him and then he feels hurt. So I criticize and criticize myself and end up without any respect for myself. Eventually he starts to come around and see things my way. That finally kills the relationship."

When we feel inadequate, it is the most difficult thing in the world to expose ourselves, to make our naked bodies vulnerable to the eyes or the touch of another. But this kind of vulnerability is the essence of intimacy. Body shyness and inhibition are major blocks to sexual enjoyment. It is nearly impossible to surrender to sexual abandon while worrying that our stomach is protruding or that our partner will see us in an unflattering angle. We suppress our feelings and deny our needs. We are shy and passive. We disown our bodies.

Many of us think that we must look a certain way before we can have a lover. We strive for the time "when I'm thin enough" or "when I get my body under control." Then we will be worthy of the pleasures of intimacy. We believe that sexuality is only permissible if we're thin, beautiful, hairless or whatever.

How sad this is, all the more tragic because it represents the secret thoughts of so many women. When you stop to think of how many of our deepest and most basic needs — the need for love, companionship, and family — have as their prerequisite the ability or willingness to form an intimate attachment, then the real tragedy becomes obvious.

•

Take a moment and close your eyes. Let yourself imagine that you are at a social gathering and you have just been introduced to a person who has all the qualities that you want in a mate. What are you feeling? What tapes are going off in your head? How are you likely to behave?

Let's take this one step further. Imagine that you have been dating this person. Imagine what it will be like for you to make love to this person for the first time. How do you feel about taking off your clothes? What do you imagine your partner is noticing about you? What are your worst fantasies?

•

If our bodies/selves are cloaked in shame and insecurity then to reveal ourselves is the last thing we want to do. And yet, to get the acknowledgment most of us need, we must take the risk to express and reveal ourselves, making ourselves vulnerable. As one woman put it:

> "I can't face people the way I am. The least I can do is to take up as little space as possible. So I am very controlled and I don't express myself. There is a lot that I want to say, but I hardly ever assert myself or take any initiative. I'm shy and reticent and I hold myself back from going after what I want or what's mine. And there's some way that I just won't give myself permission to be *me* until I look more the way I think I should."

Clothing is one way of expressing ourselves, but if we don't like our bodies or feel outsized or ill-proportioned, going shopping can be a major trauma. Most ready-to-wear clothing is only ready-to-wear if you are Brooke Shields. I call this the tyranny of the fitting room, a constant reminder that we don't fit. We must change our bodies to fit into clothes, or go naked. It is little wonder then that we rarely see our wardrobes as a means of self-expression, a way of letting the world know who we really are through our choices of color, texture, and style. More often than not our clothing becomes another way of hiding.

•

What are your special ways of not projecting yourself?

•

Advancing ourselves professionally in most fields requires that we put ourselves out there in the world complete with our full intelligence, assertiveness and competitiveness—with all our power. Most of us have not been groomed for this. We had as role models mothers who either stayed home and raised families or who went to work in jobs where they did not compete with men. Without role models and with the constant pressure on us to pursue careers, many of us feel inadequate and afraid. We question our worth and tend to shift the responsibility for our success or failure onto our poor, beleaguered bodies.

One woman came out of the cloistered environment of graduate school armed with a Masters in Business Administration. It was time to face the real world. Instead of doing so, she took refuge in her assumption that because she was overweight she simply couldn't sell herself: she didn't get a job.

Some women use their body image as an excuse to stay safe and untested while others use it as a way to stay safe and unpowerful. Many women are terrified of their own power, afraid that power spells loneliness. For others their body image is a handicap that must be compensated for by extra work: "I have to be more than perfect at my job. I work harder than three people put together and I'm always exhausted."

Another woman who would have loved to go into advertising instead works at a low paying job at a small, local newspaper. She stays away from places where she has to confront media values.

Low self-confidence keeps us from taking the kind of risks that could create the lives we want and deserve. Obsessing over our shortcomings, real or imagined, drains us of energy that could better serve us as the fuel for creativity, productivity, and self-realization.

•

Pause here and reflect on the ways that you stand in your own way, preventing your aspirations from becoming realities.

Your Body

One of the main casualties in your mind-body struggle is your body itself. All bodies need proper care to maintain good physical health. Movement and exercise are important, but proper exercise requires a real caring for the body, a program of movement performed with loving sensitivity as a gift, not as a punishment for wayward flesh. I have worked with women who have never exercised because they are embarrassed to wear exercise clothing, ashamed to be seen in a class of thin women. Other women have become so out of shape that exercise is a monumental effort. Some women take a militaristic approach, putting their bodies through Herculean ordeals in the hope of losing a few pounds or eliminating the ripples on their thighs. One woman frequently binges on several gallons of ice cream and boxes of cookies and then tries to undo the damage by going for a ten-mile run followed by two hours of strenuous gymnastics — all at 5:00 a.m.!

Body shame leads to poor posture — rounded shoulders, drooping head — which is not only unattractive but unhealthy, interfering with our ability to breathe properly. We are not giving our cells, tissues, and organs the nourishment they require. Our health suffers as does our overall energy and vitality. Poor posture also results in muscular imbalances. Many women I have worked with live with pain and minor functional complaints as if they were the premises of life rather than urgent signals. A body that is accepted and loved is listened to with a sensitive ear. In that way its needs can be known and addressed and its limits respected.

Stress is now acknowledged as one of the leading causes of disease. There are many ways to reach a dangerous level of stress: you can be a corporate executive, or an air-traffic controller, or you can be at war with your body. There is some evidence that we can actually bring on illness by holding our bodies in contempt or by disowning them. It is not unusual to find cases of women who develop cancer in their hated breasts and sexual organs and have to have them removed. In one way or another we poison ourselves with our self-rejection. Some have suggested that when we deny certain parts of our bodies or write them out of our body images, we actually create a blockage in the normal flow of energy and awareness which can eventually lead to a breakdown of the body's natural abilities to heal itself.

The women in my workshops come in every weight, shape, and size, but one thing most of them share is a distorted idea about their weight and a highly charged relationship to food. At least 90% of them perceive themselves as having eating disorders when in fact only a small proportion suffer from eating disorders in the strictly clinical sense. They are for the most part suffering not from eating disorders, but from *labelling* disorders. When fully 80% of American women have eating disorders, how can we call it a disease? Surely there are many men in our culture who engage in similar or far more extraordinary eating practices without feeling the pressure to hang a label on themselves.

Eating disorders have been woman's domain ever since Eve ate the apple. Today they are reaching epidemic proportions. The same dynamic that structures eating disorders—anorexia, bulimia, and obesity—is at work in a milder but more pervasive way in those many women who struggle with the acceptability of their bodies. They are all responding to the enormous pressure on today's woman to be thin. We are living in a world where any amount of "extra" poundage on the female body is seen as an indication of character weakness, as a sign of being out of control. Any woman carrying extra flesh on her body must lack feminine self-respect. Is it any wonder that a woman's life today revolves to such a degree around the number on her scale?

Women have been told by the medical profession and the media that their normal weight, the weight that their bodies naturally gravitate toward, is too much. And yet it is natural for us to be fatter than men. Female hormones conspire against thinness. So we feel guilty, ugly, ashamed, neurotic, self-destructive, and out of control. And naturally we want to eat more to dull the pain—food is an excellent anesthetic. Or perhaps we try to diet, starve, or otherwise whip our bodies into the desired size and shape. But the regime is too rigorous, too punitive—the body will not be so easily forced to deny its natural impulse without fighting back. Compulsive overeating takes the place of stringent dieting and the feelings of fatness, guilt, and shame return. And so the cycle goes.

•

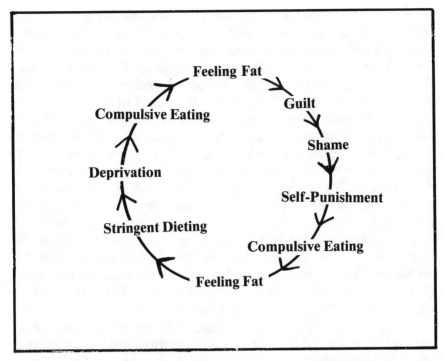

As long as women actively strive against their fleshy nature in order to fit an unnatural, external standard, how can they ever achieve a normal, healthy relationship to food?

There is a connection between eating and body image. On those days when we have been "good" and have eaten sparingly we are more likely to feel virtuous and to accept our bodies. On the other hand, when we binge we experience our bodies as swollen and engorged. Our sins are immediately visible, our guilt profound.

Time after time I hear women say, "When I feel bad, I overeat," "When I'm out of touch, I eat," "When I'm angry at myself for not controlling my eating, I punish myself by eating," "When I feel fat or bad I stuff my feelings down with food." When we are feeling bad about our bodies and ourselves we use food to soothe, punish, and numb ourselves. When we are really living in our bodies, we are far more likely to be sensitive to hunger cues and to eat appropriately in order to satisfy our needs and to stop when we are no longer hungry. When we are accepting of our bodies we are less stressed and therefore have less reason to eat to anaesthetize ourselves.

A good, healthy, positive body image is essential before we can learn how to eat and bring our weight within the proper range and keep it there. In some cases that simply means learning when we are really hungry and when we are eating for other reasons. It also means learning which foods really please and satisfy us. It may sometimes mean imposing certain food restrictions on ourselves—if we decide that a diet is necessary, our chances of succeeding and keeping the weight off are immeasurably improved if we diet lovingly.

If we are really living in our bodies and are able to accept our bodies as they are, any changes we choose to make will come from a strong base—they will be refinements, not life or death measures. If we are waiting for our bodies to be "right" before we give ourselves permission to live a full life, then we are loading the process of change with unreal expectations. We put our bodies through the rigors of deprivation and discipline and wait for the magic to happen. And it rarely does. Our knight in shining armor does not appear, a glamorous job does not drop into our laps. In fact we will really be no happier than we were before. Our outward appearance may have changed but not necessarily our body image. We will still feel fat and ungainly or whatever it was we felt beforehand.

Bodies can change much faster than body images, so we will find ourselves thin with fat body images, or firm with flabby body images. On some level we say to ourselves: "Oh, what's the use. I'm still just as awful as always. I might as well do whatever I please." So we binge or abandon our exercise program. It is absolutely crucial that we work on body image first and arrive at an accepting relationship with our bodies *before* we decide to change them.

I cannot emphasize enough how important it is to accept yourself as you are, especially if you are overweight. It is hard enough to be overweight in this culture without in addition abusing yourself. Accepting overweight is not the same thing as resigning yourself to it. In the process of learning to accept the body you have, you develop a stronger sense of yourself, with a clarity about how *you* truly want your body to be. Not what your mother wants, or your lover, or society. It will be what *you* want. If you diet to satisfy someone else, and if you have the slightest trace of rebelliousness it will come to the fore complete with anger, resentment, and the desire to sabotage your most carefully laid plans.

It is time to challenge some of the misconceptions that many of us have about overweight. Study after study has demonstrated that stereotypes of overweight people as lazy, emotionally unstable, and out of control are totally inaccurate. People who carry extra weight are just like anyone else with the same emotional ups and downs. They are no more out of control than millions of people who smoke or work too hard or drink too much or who have other ways of handling stress.

These stereotypes not only hurt fat people, they hurt anyone who thinks she has any excess fat on her body. If the scale moves up a pound, a steady stream of self-recrimination follows: "I'm out of control, I'm bad, I have no self-respect as a woman," and on and on. It is very important for us to begin challenging some of our assumptions and to realize that a pound of fat is a pound of fat and not a blight on the face of humankind.

The science and art of weight control are presently at a very primitive level of development. We really do not understand the complex problems involved in taking off weight and keeping it off. There is considerable evidence that one of the primary causes of compulsive overeating is constant dieting, and the chronic feeling of deprivation that goes with dieting. When we tip the balance in one direction and deprive our bodies of food, nature tries to restore the balance, by tipping the scale to the other extreme and making us hungrier than ever. Thus the dieting-binging-dieting cycle is born. Virtue (rigorous dieting) and vice (binging-gluttony) are natural opposites on the seesaw.

Food deprivation serves on a physiological level to lower our metabolic rate. The less dieters eat, the more slowly their bodies burn up calories, the more slowly they lose weight. And to add insult to injury, the more sluggish the metabolism, the less food it takes to put on weight. That explains the plateaus most dieters reach in the course of dieting, and the extreme difficulty in maintaining weight loss. When the weight goal is reached, it is reached in such a slow metabolic condition that the dieter must eat like a bird or exercise like a maniac in order not to undo all the hard work. Americans are fatter than ever today probably because of, not in spite of, their chronic dieting.

Scientists are discovering the individuality of every body. There is no one right way to eat, no one right way to exercise, and no one right weight. Each and every body is unique in its requirements. Some very interesting research suggests that every body has a weight range, a setpoint that is right for it. That setpoint knows nothing about what is currently in vogue. It is a stubborn and determined little mechanism with only one function, to maintain weight in the range that it considers correct.

The setpoint can be moved up or down, although it appears that it is easier to move up than down. Continued weight gain moves it up, while aerobic exercise, not dieting, can move it down, but not very easily. Recent research suggests that an aerobic program once begun, must be sustained *for life* or you will become even fatter than before. This finding emphasizes the need for very clear motives and un-shakable commitment.

What this setpoint research suggests, is that those 10-15 pounds that so many women want to lose are tenacious because we are meant to have them. And all efforts to be thinner are fighting nature and nature, as you know, is no pushover—she'll fight tooth and nail to keep our weight where she thinks it belongs. For example, several rats were subjected to a surgery destroying part of their brains, caus-ing them to eat voraciously and grow enormously fat. The scientists cut back the rats' rations to the preoperational level but instead of losing weight, the rats became even fatter than before. What hap-pened was that the operation apparently raised the rats' setpoints. If the rats could not gain weight by eating more, they would do it by bringing their metabolic rate nearly to a halt. What this means is that our bodies have wills of their own and it is not always within the realm of conscious choice to go against this wisdom. Specifically, it means that you could probably find better and more productive ways to use your energy than to spend it in the futile struggle to lose those last 10-15 pounds.

The only procedure that will work is to become more accepting of your body as it is. From that place of peace your body should begin to find its way to its right size and form. But if that does not happen, you are still left with the harmony you have worked so hard for.

II

MAKING YOUR IMAGINATION AN ALLY

The true nature of things, truth itself, can be revealed to us only by fantasy, which is more realistic than all the realisms.
Eugene Ionesco

About twenty years ago I discovered the joys of making pottery, especially throwing pots on the potter's wheel. Every day I would go to the studio to work at the wheel. Every day my technique improved and my enthusiasm grew. One weekend I was playing ball with a group of friends and sprained my little finger. Without the use of that finger my whole technique of throwing pots was off balance.

It would be at least four weeks before my finger would heal. My momentum in potting was so high I found myself spontaneously fantasizing the pot throwing process. I would imagine myself at the wheel, feeling the clay in my hands, imagining the position of my body needed to achieve just the right combination of pressure and timing. I experienced myself throwing perfect pots every time. From time to time I found myself doing this full-bodied imagining. I had no plan in mind. It was just something that happened spontaneously simply because I missed potting so much, and this was the closest I could get to it.

Four weeks passed, my finger healed, and I returned to the studio. To my amazement I discovered that my technique was light years ahead of what it had been before my injury! I could only attribute this dramatic improvement to my fantasizing.

This experience aroused in me a new respect for the powers of the imagination. I was an artist at that time in my life, and I already had a healthy regard for the importance of imagination for inspiration, but this was the first time I experienced imagination changing my behavior.

You can use your imagination to practice attitudes and behaviors that you wish to build into your life. You can expand your self image. If you can imagine it, you can live it.

What has this to do with body image? Body image is itself a special kind of image. When you have a negative body image, your mind's eye sees your body in a distorted manner and your mind's ear hears self talk saying your body is inadequate, ugly, and fat. You are held prisoner, controlled by your perception and sense of self. What better way to gain access to your tyrannical imagination than to turn it around by training your imagination to be your *ally* so that your body can become your home instead of a battlefield.

This training will take many forms in the course of this book. You will be using your imagination to tap into memories to find important information that you will need in order to understand and change your relationship to your body. Most therapeutic approaches rely on words to release you from your emotional binds. The use of imagery—the language of the unconscious and of feeling—is often a more efficient way to open locked doors to forgotten feelings and experiences. And the process is gentle: it nudges you softly—it never bulldozes its way.

All children naturally have rich and active imaginations. Most of our education has trained us to put aside the imaginal realm in favor of the rational, thinking mind. If you are an artist or a highly creative person, your imagination is probably still alive and well, but in most adults the imagination is rusty. Imaginal training will allow you to reclaim one of the most powerful resources that is at your disposal for changing your life.

The language of imagination is images. Images are pictures, sounds, feelings, tastes, and smells that you construct rather than experience directly through your senses.

•

For a moment, lift your eyes off this page and look carefully at any object near you. . . What you are doing right now is Perceiving *that object with your eyes. Now close your eyes and recreate this same object by imagining it. You can do the same thing with all of your senses although most people have one or two imaginal senses that are far easier to control than others. Try silently conversing with a friend and listening with your imaginal ears. . . imagine the feel of satin. . . the taste of lemon. . . the smell of vanilla.*

•

Every sense has its imaginal counterpart. For some of us these images will be clear and vivid. Others will have a hazy impression that the object is there and has certain characteristics. With practice your images will become clearer and more vivid and therefore more powerful.

When I ask you to imagine a sea shell or to imagine yourself walking up stairs, the process is called *guided imaging*. You are constructing very specific images. But if instead I ask you to imagine walking up stairs and entering a room where you have never been before and experiencing what is in the room, this process includes elements of *spontaneous imaging* where you simply allow images to pop into your mind as you would in a daydream. If I directed you to change the color of the room's walls and to move objects around, that would be *controlled imaging*.

As you work your way through this book you will be called upon to play with many different forms of imaging. At times your involvement will be active and dynamic while at other times it will be passive and receptive. Soon your imagination will become a true ally that you can use as a tool to help yourself not only in changing your body image but in changing many other aspects of your life as well.

Travelling in the realm of imagination is intrinsically healing because it demands a certain level of relaxation. Exploring your own flow of images allows you to glimpse what issues are pressing for further attention. Working through your emotional blocks on an imaginal level can relieve symptoms and produce personality and attitude changes. Your imagination is a piece of psychological space where you can monitor the rumblings of your subconscious mind. It is also a theater in which to rehearse behavior. If you can imagine something, you can do it.

Deeply felt imaginal experiences can change the contours of your feeling and your sense of self. Why is this? Because images are *real*. I know you have been taught that what happens in your imagination is the opposite of reality. But when you imagine something *vividly* using as many of your imaginal senses as you can muster, you are creating a *real* psychological event. You will have an example of this later when you do the exercise called *The Imaginal Body*. But for now, let's try something.

•

Imagine that you are perched on the ledge of a window twenty-three stories above street level. . . Look down at the street and see people and cars that look like ants. . . Your stomach is in your throat. . . You don't dare to move because you are balanced so precariously that any false move might send you plummeting to a sure and messy death. Take a few minutes to imagine this and do it as vividly as you can, monitoring any changes that take place in your body and emotional state.

•

Those of you who really let yourself do this exercise probably noticed that your heart was racing, fast and furiously, your breathing became shallow and perhaps your palms began to sweat — all physical signs of panic and terror. What you did was to create a genuine psycho-physical event simply by using your imagination. Can you still say that your images are not real? In a less dramatic but no less real way than our high-rise adventure, every time you imagine yourself walking upstairs your nervous system triggers movement and motor activity, however subtle, in the same muscle groups involved in walking up stairs. Your stair-walking, neuro-muscular pattern is responding even though there is no observable movement from the outside.

The same is true if you engage in an imaginary confrontation with someone with whom you have unfinished emotional business. If you do it vividly, using your full-bodied imagination, you will be setting off the same reactions in your psyche and nervous system that you would in a real confrontation. Such an encounter can perform two healing functions. It can serve as a rehearsal that can move you closer to a face-to-face encounter with that person so that you can clear up your unfinished business. It can function also at a much subtler level. Sometimes it is not possible to talk directly to that person. Perhaps she or he is no longer in your life, or such an encounter would be much too risky. Full-bodied imaging can convince your subconscious mind that a "real" confrontation has taken place and a shift in your perspective can result.

In other words, we can do profound psychological rearranging without leaving the safety of our inner space. Using images in this way can heal old psychological wounds that are standing in your way. That is what this process is all about: clearing away the emotional and attitudinal debris that keeps you engaged in battle with your body, that keeps you from a clear perception of who you are, or your body image. You can make use of your power and reclaim your body.

Section 2
Tools for Transformation

III
KNOWING
WHAT YOU WANT

*Before you begin a thing remind yourself that difficulties and
delays quite impossible to foresee are ahead. . . You can only
see one thing clearly and that is your goal. Form a mental
vision of that and cling to it through thick and thin.*
                                    Kathleen Norris

This work is about making important choices: how you choose to
feel about your body; what kind of body you choose to have; how
you choose to talk to your body and to yourself about your body;
what you choose to take in from outside sources; what you choose
not to take in. Perhaps you are not accustomed to seeing these as
choices but as givens. Looked at closely, they are simply ideas that
you have swallowed whole: you haven't spit out those pieces that are
indigestible—having nothing to do with you.

Now is the time to become clear about what it is *you choose* for
yourself in your relationship with your body. These choices will then
become your goals. With your sights set, any obstacles along the way
can be more easily overcome.

EXERCISE 1
Making Choices

Part 1
1. Sit comfortably, close your eyes and relax.
2. Tune in to your experience of being in your body right now. How
are you *feeling* in your body right now?. . . How are you talking to
yourself about your body right now?
3. Write down the words and phrases that came up for you.

4. Try each one on for size by saying each of them aloud in a way that acknowledges that this is how you feel in and about your body right now, *e.g.,* "I am heavy and sluggish," "I am tight," etc. After saying each one, pause and reflect on your feeling response to each statement.

5. Acknowledge to yourself that this is the point from which you are embarking on the journey toward wholeness.

Part 2

1. Close your eyes and relax again.

2. Now go into your imagination and discover how you really would *like* to *feel* in and about your body. Do not think of how you would like to look, but how you would like to feel, say light and easy.

3. Write down the words and phrases that came up for you.

4. Try each one on for size, first by letting yourself really feel each quality, then by saying each word or phrase aloud in a way that takes ownership of the feeling as if it were already true for you, for example, "I can move with a feeling of lightness and ease," etc.

5. Assemble these feelings into a *set of choices* that you wish to make true for yourself as you live your life in your body.

6. Enter this *set of choices* on the Statement of Intent that follows.

Worksheet
Statement of Intent

Transforming Body Image is a process of awakening to my own beauty, a beauty as unique as I am.

I, _____, am in process of changing my relation to my body.

This is what I choose for myself:

1.

2.

3.

4.

5.

And I deserve it.

Guiding Words

Please make a copy of the Statement of Intent and mount it on your wall in a prominent place so that it will jog your memory about what it is you want for yourself and your body. After all, you are doing this work so that you will one day be able to feel the way you choose about your body. You may find as you progress through these exercises that you become even clearer about these choices. When that happens, feel free to add, delete, or refine any of the chosen qualities that you have written on your Statement of Intent.

I want to underline one idea because it is extremely important for your transformation: your *feelings* in and about your body are what really count here, not the way your body *looks* from the outside. Focusing on the outer form of your body makes you an *object* to yourself. It takes you outside of your body. (I am not saying that the outer form of your body is irrelevant. What I am saying is that the outer form of your body can be lovely, but unless your inner feelings support that experience of loveliness you will be blind to it.)

•

Here are some ways to use your *set of choices:*
1. Create out of it a Feeling Meditation — let yourself feel all of these qualities using all of your imaginal senses. Do this for several minutes first thing in the morning and last thing at night. This will help you stay in touch with your goals.
2. Do your Feeling Meditation for a minute or two before and after doing any of the exercises in this book.
3. Do your Feeling Meditation any time you wish to feel clear and positive in and about your body.

IV
TRAINING YOUR IMAGINAL MUSCLES

As a child your imagination was the liveliest part of your mental equipment but, unless you are a veteran daydreamer or are actively involved in some artistic or creative work, your imagination has probably grown rusty.

Working with the imagination requires a very special mental state combining relaxation with alertness. Deep relaxation allows you to be receptive to the spontaneous images that freely come and go. Images are delicate creations—the quieter and more relaxed you are, the more sensitive you can be to the images your imagination presents to you. However, you should have some degree of alertness so that you can exercise control over your imagery. You will be asked at times to be open and receptive and at other times to manipulate your images. Before you begin an exercise, find a quiet place where you will not be interrupted.

Because we are all different we have our favorite ways of relaxing. Perhaps you have already found one that works for you. If not, hopefully one of these will appeal to you. In general when doing the exercises please sit in a chair or on the floor. You want to find a way to be comfortable enough to relax, but not so comfortable that you will fall asleep.

EXERCISE 2
Learning To Relax

RELAXXXXXXX
1. Stretch your body like a cat just awakening from a nap. . . And then sit comfortably so that your body is well supported. . .
2. Breathe naturally for 5 cycles of inbreath/outbreath. While you are breathing, scan your body for any areas that are uncomfortable and in need of rearranging. . .

3. Turn your attention back to your breathing. Watch your breath go in and out — don't try to change it, simply watch your breath breathe itself. . .

4. Breathe in and mentally say the word "Relax" as you exhale. . . Repeat this cycle for five minutes or until you feel relaxed.

Cleansing Breath Relaxation*

1. Turn your attention back to your breathing and watch your breath go in and out — don't try to change it, simply watch your breath breathe itself. . .

2. Now imagine that you have a nose on the bottom of both feet. . . Picture and feel the air coming in through the bottoms of your feet as you inhale. . . With each inhalation, pull the air up all the way from your feet — through your ankles, legs, and body, through your lungs and exhale through your mouth. Do this several times. . .

3. As you breathe in, actually feel the pull of drawing the air through the cells and tissues of your body. . . Imagine debris, ashes, or dried leaves swirling up with each breath — debris representing any emotional or physical distraction in the form of tension, fear, discomfort, etc. . . . They are being swept up and released from your cells and tissues with every deep exhalation. . . See it leaving your body in clouds. . . Experience this with all your senses and continue for several minutes.

4. Now try breathing in from some other part of your body that catches your attention, pulling the air in through the cells and tissues of that part of your body, sweeping up noise and releasing it from your body as you exhale. . .

5. Continue this cleansing breath, drawing the air in through any part of your body in which you find "noise" that impedes your total relaxation.

---

* Adapted from "Noise-Removal Breathing" from Win and Susan Wenger's *Your Limitless Inventing Machine*. Gaithersburg, MD: Psychogenics Press, 1979.

Some Image Relaxations

Candle in the Sun
1. Stretch your body like a cat just awakening from a nap. . . Then sit comfortably so that your body is well supported.
2. Breathe naturally for 5 cycles of inbreath/outbreath and while you are breathing scan your body for any areas that are uncomfortable and in need of rearranging. . .
3. Turn your attention back to your breathing and begin to watch your breath go in and out—don't try to change it, simply watch your breath breathe itself. . .
4. Imagine that you are a candle sitting in a hot, sunny window. . . As the rays of sunshine beat down on you, *feel* yourself begin to melt. . . Imagine that your concerns and tensions are dropping away as the droplets of wax roll down the side of the candle. . . *feel* yourself melting into a state of soft, deep relaxation. . . Let go and give in to the warmth of the sun and the inevitability of your melting as you release all mental and bodily tension and sink into a state of soft, deep relaxation.

Cloud Ride
1. Stretch your body like a cat just awakening from a nap. Then sit comfortably so that your body is well supported. . .
2. Breathe naturally for 5 cycles of inbreath/outbreath and while you are breathing scan your body for any areas that are uncomfortable and in need of rearranging. . .
3. Turn your attention back to your breathing and watch your breath go in and out—don't try to change it, simply watch your breath breathe itself. . .
4. Imagine a beautiful clear blue sky with several puffy, white clouds floating along with the air currents. . . Hop aboard a cloud and let yourself float along totally supported by the soft and enveloping cloud. . . You have nothing to do now but relax, float, and enjoy the ride.

•

The more you practice these relaxation sequences the easier they will be for you to do. Find one sequence that you like and stick with it. Now you are ready to flex your imaginal muscles and reclaim that powerhouse, your imagination.

Whatever you can see with your eyes you can "see" with your imaginal eyes. This also holds true for all your other senses. You have imaginal ears that "hear" the sounds in your inner environment, and an imaginal body that "feels" sensations and experiences feeling states on an emotional level. We will exercise most of the imaginal senses, but three will predominate: seeing, hearing, and feeling/touching. The more vividly you can use your imagination—that is, the more present you are in your fantasy and the sharper your imaginal senses are—the more powerful will be your experience and the deeper your transformation. Full-bodied imagining will be your ticket to body-mind health.

EXERCISE 3
Sensory Remembering

1. Please sit comfortably, close your eyes and relax.
2. Imagine yourself in some room or interior space that is very familiar, perhaps your bedroom or your kitchen. . . .
3. Look around you, carefully noticing details of shape and color. Perhaps you will see it all at once, or part by part. . . Look up at the ceiling and down at the floor. Notice the rugs, the arrangement of furniture and objects. . . How many doors and windows are there in the room?. . . What color are the walls and furnishings?. . . See if you can change the color of the walls and certain objects in the room. . .
4. Listen carefully a moment and notice what sounds are characteristic of this space. . . Perhaps it is the sound of traffic outside the window, or footsteps in the hallway, or the hum of the refrigerator. Take a moment to tune in with your imaginal ears. . .
5. Walk around the room and experience fully the sensations in your body as you move—notice the pressure of your feet against the floor, the sound that your feet are making, the feel of the air on your skin. . .

6. As you move through the room reach out with your imaginal hands and touch the objects in the room—the walls, woodwork, fabrics—all the surfaces and textures. . . Now move some of these objects around. . .

7. With your imaginal nose sniff the air and notice the smells in the air. . .

8. Let the image of the room go. . . See an imaginary curtain close on that scene. Rest a moment in the dark. . .

9. And now the curtain opens on a recent scene in which you had some very pleasant physical experience with good physical sensations such as eating a delicious meal, dancing, receiving a wonderfully sensuous massage, or making love. Take a moment to choose this scene and recreate it. . . Now experience moving into this scene until you can *feel* the sensations as if they were happening to you right now. . . Enjoy the pleasurable sensations noticing also the sights, sounds, smells, or tastes attached to this experience. . .

10. Prepare yourself to leave your imaginal space/time and to return to this place and time.

Worksheet

1. Were you able to do this exercise? If not, what difficulties did you have?

2. Describe some of your most vivid images in the present tense as if they were happening to you right now.

3. Which of your imaginal senses are the most vivid?

4. Which are the least vivid?

5. Comments.

Guiding Words

Most people find that they are far more facile with some imaginal senses than they are with others. Keep practicing until you feel comfortable at least with your imaginal eyes, ears and touch/feeling sense. Imaginal smell and taste are less important to this process.

Don't expect your imaginal senses to be as vivid as your real senses. It is the rare individual whose imagination produces truly clear and life-like images. Many people, myself included, cannot actually see or hear distinct images but "know" that the images are there.

When doing such quiet inner work, it is not uncommon for your attention to wander or for you even to fall asleep. The more at home you become with this way of working, the easier it will be for you to keep your attention focused. If you do fall asleep, ask yourself whether you are too relaxed or genuinely in need of rest. Perhaps falling asleep in the middle of these exercises may be a signal that there is something in the process you would rather avoid. Try to be honest. No matter what the reason is, do the sequence again until you can stay awake throughout.

It is not necessary to be a perfectionist about your imagining. Just keep practicing Sensory Remembering and the next exercise until you have confidence in your own imaginal agility. By the end of this book imaging will be second nature to you.

In the next exercise I will be asking you to do some things which may seem silly. They will tone your imaginal muscles and bring you closer to being a full-bodied imager, one who uses all of her senses in the imaging. The more of yourself you bring to this work, the more powerful your changes will be.

Your body image exists on many levels: neurological, mental, and emotional. The part of your body image that you are about to experience involves your nervous system or, more specifically, your kinesthetic sense. It is your brain and nervous system that are ultimately responsible for your kinesthetic sense, that sense which lets you know how to move your body, where your body is in space, and where your body parts are in relation to one another. It also lets you feel sensations and responses in your body. It is your felt sense; without it you would not be able to move or function in the physical world.

Exercising your imaginal body means exercising your nervous system. When you move an imaginal limb you trigger the same nerve pathways as you do when you move a real limb. This next exercise is central to changing your body image.

EXERCISE 4
The Imaginal Body

1. Please stand up and find a space where you will have room to spread your arms later. Close your eyes so that you can turn your attention inward. Notice how your body feels as you stand. . . Notice the alignment of your body. . . The feeling of your feet meeting the floor. . . Your sense of being grounded. . . Notice your body in relation to space. . . Notice the extent to which you feel you are in your body. . . Remember how you are now as a reference point for later.

2. Turn your attention to your head and neck. Move your chin toward your chest and back again. Repeat this several times, up and down, until you grasp the sensations involved in doing this act. . . Memorize these feelings. Now do the same movement with your *imaginal* head and neck. In your imagination move your chin toward your chest and back, trying to do it as vividly as you did with your real head and neck. Do this several times. If you need to refresh your memory, do the movement again with your real body. (Don't be surprised if you feel tiny muscular contractions as you exercise your imaginal body. You are activating your nervous system merely through the *intention* of moving it.)

3. Alternate the movement between your real head and neck and your imaginal head and neck, several times. . . Let go of this movement.

4. Now raise both real arms to shoulder height, out to the sides. Slowly lower and raise them several times until you can grasp and memorize the sensations involved in this movement. . . Do the same movement now with your imaginal arms trying to do it just as vividly. . .

5. Alternate between your real and imaginal arms several times, first raising and lowering the one and then the other, refreshing your memory if you need to. . .

6. Now you will really need to concentrate. Raise your real right arm and your imaginal left arm *at the same time.* Lower them. Then reverse it and raise your real left arm and your imaginal right arm. Lower them and reverse it again. Repeat this several times. . . Lower both arms. (Don't worry if this is confusing. Take your time and realize that you are asking your brain and nervous system to stretch and expand. Keep trying. To make it easier, with your eyes closed,

slowly raise your real right arm, and then hold it there. In your imagination raise your left arm. Now bring them both down to your
side simultaneously. As the process becomes easier, gradually col-
lapse the time element until you are raising your real right arm and
your imaginal left arm together.)

7. Now raise your real right arm and imaginal left arm and bring
them together in front of you. Clap them together several times. . .
Reverse your arms and clap them again several times. . . Lower your
arms, rest a moment and center yourself. . .

8. Begin to walk forward four or five steps. . . Reverse direction and
walk backwards. . . Repeat this several times. . . Now walk forward
and back with your imaginal body, several times. . .

10. Walk forward with your real body while you walk backwards
with your imaginal body. . . Then reverse it so that you are walking
forward with your imaginal body while your real body walks
backward. . . Repeat this sequence several times.

11. Rest a moment and note the feelings in your body.

12. Make a space — a radius of several feet in front of you. Now with
your real body jump into that space in front of you. Jump back. Do
the same thing with your imaginal body, forward and back. Now
with the real body. Real body again. Imaginal body forward and
back. Now with the real body. Real body again. Imaginal body, forward and back. Finally, jump forward with your imaginal body and
stay there. Then, jumping as high as you can, jump with your real
body *into* your imaginal body.

13. Stand quietly for a moment and compare what you are feeling
now in your body to what you felt in the beginning of this exercise.
And now walk around naturally and experience your body in motion.

Worksheet

1. Were you able to do this exercise? If not, describe your difficulties.
2. Describe your experience of doing this exercise as if it were happening to you right now. Include any surprises, discoveries, insights,
etc.
3. How are you feeling in and about your body right now?
4. Comments.

Guiding Words

Those of us who are locked in struggle with our bodies tend to have a weak or undeveloped kinesthetic sense. It is difficult to be kinesthetically grounded in our bodies when we are disconnected from them. So please don't be discouraged if this exercise is difficult for you. It demands considerable concentration.

One woman, Francine, wrote:

> "I had difficulty in feeling my real body as it moved; therefore I had difficulty in feeling my imaginal body move. The kinesthetic sense is something I lack. . . . Because it was hard for me—I met with more resistance. Yet, I am excited because I feel this kinesthetic sense of myself is in large part what makes me feel so unreal and alienated from my body."

This is a very important point. Your kinesthetic and visual senses are the two most important senses needed to change your body image.

This exercise can be confusing. Should you concentrate on your left side or your right? On your real or your imaginal body? Obviously, it is very difficult, if not impossible, to be in two places at the same time. That is the beauty of this exercise. To do all that it asks, you must be acting from your center, not the left or right, real or imaginal. This explains Annette's response, typical of so many who have done this process:

> "I am exhilarated by actually jumping into my own body. It feels good to be *in* my body. I enjoy walking around and experiencing the sensations. Before I began I experienced my body as being like a rock, heavy and lifeless. Afterwards I felt I was alive inside my body. I have a sense of being attuned—in my body. It's a feeling of integration and wholeness."

V
GETTING TO KNOW YOUR BODY IMAGE

As conscious human beings we possess the unique capacity to see ourselves, to stand back and judge. We are the only creatures on earth who can be *objects* to ourselves. When we look at ourselves in the mirror we are both subject and object, perceiver and perceived. Out of our perceptions and experience of ourselves we have constructed a self image. And out of our perceptions and experience of our bodies we have constructed a body image.

Your body image is a very subtle and complex aspect of yourself, that piece of psychological space where your body and mind come together. It is dynamic and changeable. Elements of it are different from one day to the next; yet it is also stable. You probably have notions about your body that have been fixed for many years. It is conscious. At times you are painfully aware of your experience in your body. But it is also unconscious — you do not have to stop and think about how to move your legs to walk. You have many beliefs about your body that motivate your behavior but which are not available to your conscious mind.

Your body image is not the same as your physical body. It is the way *you* see and experience your body, not necessarily how the world sees it — although how others experience your body can be very strongly influenced by the verbal and non-verbal messages you communicate about and through your body. Body sensations and your knowledge of where your body parts are in relation to each other and in relation to space contribute to your body image.

Your body image is experienced on a visual level, how you see your body; a kinesthetic level, your felt sense of being in your body; and an auditory level, how you think about and talk to yourself about your body. You will probably find that one or two of these levels need more rearranging. Perhaps you *feel* comfortable in your body, but thinking about how you look to others depresses you. Or it could be the other way around. Maybe you *look* fine to yourself, but you catch yourself *saying* horrible things to yourself about your body.

Your body image encompasses your ideas, feelings, attitudes, and values about your body. Every time you see yourself in the mirror or catch a fleeting glance reflected in a store window, every time you look directly at areas of your body, what you see is colored by your body image.

EXERCISE 5
Body Scanning

This exercise is a way of mapping your subjective, felt experience of your body, as well as the relationship of body parts to each other and to the environment. It is also a way of mapping the emotional life of your body. The exercise is divided into two parts. It is up to you whether you choose to do them in one go or two. I will be asking you questions to which there are no right answers. The answers should come from your internal experience rather than from your ideas. It is a special and very important kind of knowing. The more times that you do this exercise, the better you will get to know your body and body image. Areas that are uncharted territories will become more clearly defined, less subject to distortion. As your kinesthetic sense develops you will function more fully in everything you do.

NOTE: Please read each step and then close your eyes and go inside yourself for your answers.

Part 1

1. Lie down directly on the floor with your legs uncrossed, arms down by your sides. Notice how you are feeling in your body. . . Begin to pay attention to your breathing, simply noticing how this happens for you. Don't try to change anything, but rather trust that, after all these years, your breath knows how to breathe itself. Just allow yourself to breathe naturally and notice. . .

— What parts of your body move when you breathe?
— In what order are they moving?
— Are you breathing through your mouth or through your nose?

—Are you inhaling all the way, or is there some restriction that prevents you from taking a full in-breath?

—When you exhale, do you empty your lungs completely?

—Follow your breath and use it as a means to getting to know the inner areas of your body.

2. Try to sense how much of the surface of your body is present in your awareness. Scan your surface to discover which areas of your body's surface are clear and which are vague or missing entirely from your awareness. . .

3. Bring your attention now to the way that your body is lying on the floor.

—How are you feeling on the floor? Light? Heavy? Free? Constricted? How is it for you right now?

—Sense the contact that your back makes with the floor. Is it the same on the right as it is on the left?

—Notice those places where you are feeling pressure. . . Move your awareness from your heels to your head, noticing those parts of your body where you accept the support of the floor and therefore feel contact or pressure. . .

—Notice where in your body there is no contact with the floor: In your mind's eye imagine the size and shape of the spaces between your neck and the floor; the tips of your shoulders and the floor; between your shoulder blades; the small of your back; your knees, ankles, and wrists.

—With your hand (disturbing the way you are lying on the floor as little as possible) explore the spaces behind your neck, and the small of your back to see if they are as you sensed them to be. . .

4. Turn your attention to experience your body as a whole.

—If the ceiling were to be lowered right now, which part of your body would it touch first? Your breasts? Your nose? Your tummy? Your toes?

—How wide are you? Internally sense the width of your body, finding where you are widest. Where are you narrowest?

—Discover those places where you carry the most and least flesh.

5. Relying on your internal sense and not your memory, sense the width of your head. . . Then represent that width holding both hands directly over your face. Gently lower your hands to your face and check the accuracy of your sensing.

6. Try to sense the width of your hips. . . Represent that distance with both of your hands, holding them just over your hips. Lower them carefully, disturbing their relationship as little as possible, and

once again check the accuracy of your sensing against the true width of your hips.

7. Now experience your body as an integrated whole. . . Say to yourself the following, inserting your own name:

"This is my body. This is where I, _____, live." Feel the impact of these words on you. Say it again.

Worksheet

1. How is your body feeling right now? Has it changed merely from paying attention to it?

2. Describe your experience as if it were happening right now (including any reactions, surprises, questions, and feelings aroused by the process).

3. What areas of your body image are clearest and which are faint or missing?

4. Are your assessments of size and shape accurate or distorted?

5. Note any difficulties you had in doing this exercise.

6. Comments.

Part 2

1. Lie down, relax and notice how you are feeling in your body right now. . .

2. Scan your body to discover where you store emotions. To locate an emotion it is often helpful to imagine a situation where you felt that emotion and then to notice where in your body you experience that feeling.

— Where in your body does your anger reside?
— Where in your body does your love reside?
— Where in your body does your guilt reside?
— Where in your body does your shame reside?
— Where in your body does your fear reside?
— Where in your body does your mother reside?
— Where in your body does your father reside?
— Where in your body does your joy reside?

3. Scan your body for any other areas that hold some emotional charge or where you feel blocked or stuck. See if you can discover what messages these areas hold for you. Take each one in turn and ask yourself what each area would say if it could speak. See how you want to respond to each one. . .

4. Now experience your body as an integrated whole. Say to yourself the following, inserting your own name:

"This is my body. This is where I, _____, live." Feel the impact of these words on you. Say it again.

Worksheet

1. How is your body feeling right now?

2. Describe your experience as if it were happening right now (including any reactions, surprises, questions, and feelings aroused by the process).

3. Draw a map of your body locating areas where you found emotions or blockages.

4. What messages did your body have for you?

5. Note any difficulties you had in doing this exercise.

6. Comments.

Guiding Words

Body scanning is a way of becoming kinesthetically grounded.

It can change the way you experience your body from an amorphous blur to a clear image. This clarity is needed for a healthy mind-body relationship. Body scanning is also a first step in opening communication with your body, providing information about needs, blockages, and emotional states.

I recommend that you do this exercise several times. Each repetition will enrich your vocabulary of kinesthetic experience, reducing the potential for your distorting body image as well as making your emotions more available to you.

Francine learned a great deal about her body image and herself:

> "I am surprised how dominant the upper half of my body seems, especially my face and shoulders. When the ceiling comes down it touches my nose first. From the waist down, my body drifts away but looms large in my mind. I am surprised (and laugh) when I measure the size of my hips—they are much smaller than I imagined. They feel good to me. My hands linger on them with more acceptance. I am more accurate with the sense of the size of my head and facial features though I underestimate the fullness of my lips. I feel that I purse my lips a lot with disgust and restraint and that my lips have therefore shrunk. When I ask what messages my body parts have for me, my back feels pain and says, 'Please don't overload me.' My right ovary is also in pain and says, 'I'm aching. I'm part of your femaleness. Have you forgotten me? I am part of your link to life, to cycles, to birth and death.' My throat is blocked and says, 'I want to cry. I want to shout. I want to sing. Please don't throttle me. I want to express myself.' My abdominal/genital area says, 'Please don't hate me, I'm not bad.' My breasts are numb and they say, 'I wish I were a little girl again.'"

Francine's story makes it easy to see how feelings and ideas about our bodies can create distortion in our body images. It also shows how much rich and important information is available to us if we take the time to attend to our bodies' messages. Often feelings that we refuse to acknowledge or express will be readable in our body, so that the more in touch with our body we become, the more we can be in touch with our feelings. Identifying body feelings takes practice, so be patient if the first attempt yields only sketchy clues.

Body Scanning asks you to do a very special kind of attending to your body, a quiet, fine-tuned, mindful attention full of noticing and empty of judgment. Practicing makes it possible for you to carry this non-judgmental attention into your daily interactions with your body and with everything else in your life as well.

For most women, the visual level of the body image experience is the most distorted and prone to judgment. When we look into a mirror, we do not necessarily see what is there. Instead we probably see an image laden with past associations, feelings, criticisms, unrealized aspirations, and many other things that have little or nothing to do with what the mirror presents to us.

We have very little opportunity to see ourselves as we really are. The mirror image is reversed and usually posed. The camera freezes us into static postures and adds weight to our frames. We can see certain parts of our bodies directly by looking down at our torsos and limbs, but we see them distorted by foreshortening.

We form distorted judgments of what we look like and over time these judgments become unconscious and habitual. By making these feelings and judgments conscious and explicit, we can confront them and change them.

EXERCISE 6
Imaginary Mind-Mirror

1. Sit comfortably, close your eyes and relax.
2. In your imagination, go where there is a full length, three-way mirror. Stand in front of the mirror, fully clothed, and look at yourself from all angles. Study the image in the mirror very carefully and as objectively as you can. Pretend that you are seeing you for the first time. See if you can look at yourself with an attitude of discovery.
3. If you were seeing this person in the mirror for the first time, what messages would you receive from looking at her?
   — What can you tell about this person from the way she holds herself?
   — What can you tell about this person from the expression on her face?
   — What can you tell about this person from the way she dresses?
   — How does this person in the mirror appear to feel about herself and her body?
4. In your imagination, take off your clothes. Look at your naked body in the mirror with the same sense of discovery.
   — Is there any shift in the way you are holding yourself?
   — What feelings come up for you as you look at your naked body?
   — Do you feel pleased? Ashamed? Vulnerable? What?
   — What judgments do you form as you look at your naked body?
5. What areas of your body do you focus on? What areas do you avoid or gloss over?
6. What do you like about your body? What do you dislike?
7. Take a closer look at your imaginal reflection from the front and, as you observe each part of your body, notice carefully the feelings, judgments and any other bits of self-analysis that come up for you.

Acknowledge them and see if you can let them go and move on.

- How do you feel about your face and head? Notice your hair, eyes, nose, mouth, neck, and skin.
- How do you feel about your body skin? Notice its color, texture, and tone.
- How do you feel about your torso? Notice your shoulders, breasts, waist, belly, hips, and genitals.
- How do you feel about your arms and hands? Your legs and feet?
- How do you feel about the lines and curves of your body?

8. Turn around and notice how your body looks from the side. Notice your judgments and ask yourself how attached you are to them.

- Notice your posture: the way your head sits on your neck, the curve of your back.
- Notice the line of your buttocks where it meets your waist, and again where it meets your thighs.
- Notice the curve of your belly and the shape of your breasts.
- Notice the shape of your legs.

9. Now turn so that you can see the imaginal rear view of your body.

- Notice the way you are standing.
- Notice what parts are clear to you and what parts are vague.
- How do you feel about what you are seeing?

10. Turn and face yourself. Look into your reflection, and acknowledge to yourself: "This is my body. This is where I, _____, live."

Worksheet

1. What are you feeling right now? How are you feeling about your body?
2. Describe your experience of looking at your reflection as if it were happening right now (include observations, surprises, feelings, judgments, and impressions).
3. What self judgments are you willing to relinquish?
4. What self judgments are difficult to relinquish?
5. Note any difficulties you had in doing this exercise.
6. Comments.

Guiding Words

Chances are that your first attempts at this exercise yielded negative material. If you had only positive feelings about your body, you wouldn't be reading this book. It is this negative material that you must ferret out so that you see clearly what you do to yourself most of the time.

Barbara had a very active judge.

> "I see the things I don't like but don't spend much time and energy looking and thinking about the body parts I do like. Sometimes in the mirror I feel my body is screaming out 'ugly' because I can't keep my body in sync with my ideal mental image of how I should look. I sometimes come closer, but some small imperfection yells out, 'I'm here,' so that I, as well as everyone else, can see it plainly as a blemish."

We are fiercely committed to seeing ourselves in a negative light and making certain that everyone else does also. Peggy's vigilant judge was always quick to "overcrowd (her) good feelings with negative statements." It became clear to her that she was heavily invested in maintaining a negative body image to reaffirm her position that she was an unlovable, unacceptable failure.

Looking at herself in this careful way, Kathryn realized something important.

> "At first I felt nothing. Then I began to really look at myself, the curves, texture, contour, lines of the past. . . I began to feel that my denial of my body was a way to continue the denial of myself. . . that an affirmation of my body was an affirmation of myself. As long as I could hold on to a negation of my body, refuse to value and appreciate its beauty and goodness, it was easy to negate myself, continue the self-hatred, self-pity, and self-denial that filled my life, distorting my relationship with myself and others. I am beginning to see and feel quite clearly that I am my body and to love my body is to love myself."

It may make you squirm to see what you do to yourself. Growth usually requires some degree of discomfort before you are ready to let go of self-defeating attitudes and behaviors. This exercise is the beginning of a long process of identifying the many voices that live inside you. Right now your inner critics outnumber and outvoice your inner fans. This balance will begin to shift as you become willing to confront and even to silence your judges.

The next exercise will help you reach even more deeply into your subconscious mind. As you go through this sequence, see if you can be open to whatever images appear spontaneously. Try not to force the images. They may be surprising or confusing but are probably accurate expressions of your inner reality. Above all, try to trust your own process. Your subconscious mind will present you with no more and no less than you are ready to deal with.

EXERCISE 7
Opening Doors

1. Sit comfortably, close your eyes and relax.
2. Experience yourself walking outdoors. It's a lovely day. Notice the color of the sky. . . The temperature of the air against your skin. . . Feel the ground under your feet and your body in motion. . . Pay attention to any sights, sounds, and fragrances that emerge along the way. . .
3. Off in the distance you notice a building. As you approach it at closer range, you see that it is a house. Keep walking until you are standing in front of the house. . .
4. Walk around the house so that you can see it from all angles. . . Notice what the house looks like, the condition of the exterior, size, shape, color, architectural style and any other details. . .
5. Notice how the house relates to its surroundings. . . Is it landscaped? Does it have a garden? Are there other buildings nearby?
6. How do you feel about this house? Do you like it? Do you like its style and the statement it makes from the outside? What don't you like about it?

Worksheet

1. Describe yourself in the present tense the way you described the house: for example, "I am large and stately," "I am well built but in need of paint," "I am small and unpretentious in the middle of the forest," etc.
2. In what ways does your house image fit or not fit your body image or your sense of yourself?
3. What are your feelings about this house?

•

7. Return to your image of the house and walk up to the front door. Place your hand on the doorknob and think of opening the door and stepping over the threshold into yourself. . . What feelings come up for you?. . . Acknowledge them and then open the door.

8. Walk into the house and spend several minutes exploring the interior, letting your images come as freely and spontaneously as possible, without judgment or forcing. Stay in touch with your feelings as you explore. . .

9. Look around the house until you find a hallway with doors on both sides. . . Begin to walk down the hall until you find a door with the words, "Body Room" written on it. . . Place your hand on the knob and once again contact and acknowledge your feelings as you anticipate opening the door and entering the room. . .

10. Open the door and enter your "Body Room." Using all your imaginal senses, let your images of the interior of the room come as freely as possible without judging or forcing them. Spend several minutes in your "Body Room" exploring its contents, all the while staying in touch with whatever feelings come up for you. . .

11. Choose one object or quality or aspect of the room that especially attracts your attention. Go up to it and ask it: "What message do you have for me about my relationship with my body?" Now identify with the object — really become it — and respond to the question as if you were speaking *as* the object. . . Return to yourself. . . Thank the object for its help.

12. Repeat step No. 11 with any other objects or aspects of the room that feel attractive or significant to you.

Worksheet

1. Reflect on each object until you understand its meaning in relation to the way you experience your body:

   a. How are you (or your body) like this object? What part of you does it represent?

   b. What associations do you have with this object?

   c. How would you translate the message the object had for you into an understanding of the work you need to do with your body image?

•

13. Return to your image of the "Body Room" and stand back so you can survey it as a whole. . . Reflect on how you would like this room to be. What changes would you like to make in the room?. . . Take a few minutes and carry out these changes using all your imaginal senses as vividly as possible as if in a speeded up film. . .

14. Now prepare to leave your "Body Room." Take one last look and turn to leave, closing the door behind you, knowing that this is a door that you can open any time you wish to have a symbolic reading of your relationship with your body.

Worksheet

1. What have you learned about your body image from doing this exercise?

2. What sense do you make out of the images you chose? What do they have to teach you?

3. Describe your feelings upon opening doors. Do they have any relationship to your feelings about doing this work on body image?

4. How would you translate the changes you made in the room into changes you want to make in your relationship with your body?

5. Note any difficulties you had in doing this exercise.

6. Comments.

Guiding Words

A house is often thought of as an archetypal symbol of the self and the body. Opening symbolic doors can give accurate and sometimes surprising information about the self/body image. A symbol is able to burrow under the surface without arousing the same degree of resistance as a direct approach. Working symbolically can be a very powerful way of bringing what is hidden or partially hidden about ourselves into the open.

In *Opening Doors* you have tapped into information regarding the way you present yourself on the outside, how you experience yourself inside, and what is going on in your body image. Our inner symbolism is very fluid. If you do this exercise several times (and I recommend that you do), the symbolism will probably change. These different images do not cancel each other out — they add up to a richer understanding of this very subtle and complex piece of inner space, your body image.

It is often striking how accurately this exercise can reveal conflicts. Patricia saw her house as a

> "castle, cold, large, and empty. I am surrounded by water, and a small, treacherous bridge leads to the iron gates. Vines entangle the house and there are tall, green trees all around the back. The sign says, 'Beware — Do Not Enter'. . . This perfectly describes how I think and feel about myself lately."

Patricia *is* difficult to see and dangerous to approach. Her inner experience is of space, cold and empty.

It is not unusual to have an exterior and interior that convey very different qualities. Allison's house was a

> "large, urban apartment building, neat, orderly, but cold, except that each apartment is warm, cozy, and safe. . . I think I project myself as being large, self-assured and solid like the apartment building. And the way I relate to people is sometimes detached and impersonal. However, inside the various apartments there are a lot of feelings."

I suggested that Allison have a dialogue between the cold outside and the warm inside so that she could see what she was trying to accomplish by maintaining such an exterior. This is a useful technique when dealing with contradictions in imagery. Allison't image is also revealing of the way she detaches herself from her feelings by compartmentalizing them in separate apartments.

The way you feel just before opening doors to your imagery often relates to the way you are approaching this work. In a sense, beginning this work is like walking across a threshold into yourself. Some of you will open doors with gusto and excited anticipation, while others will feel some mixture of willingness, apprehension, fear, resistance, and open refusal. Whatever you experience is fine. Simply acknowledge that this is where you stand and try to decide where you choose to go from there.

The interior of your "Body Room" holds questions and answers for you about your current relationship with your body. This rich information may be couched in obscure symbols or may be blatantly obvious. It is valuable for you to come to your own interpretations of the images you have chosen. By using the technique of identifying with your images you can begin to understand them from the inside, within the context of your own set of meanings.

It is not unusual to find the "Body Room" dark or empty. An empty room is not devoid of information. Sometimes it holds the key to knowing what is *missing* in your relationship with your body, or in your knowledge of this relationship. Sometimes it means simply that it is premature for you to receive certain information. Even a dark or empty room has structural features, walls, doors, floors, etc., that can be felt, that might hold messages if you seek them. Occasionally darkness or emptiness is a signal that something will emerge from the darkness if you hold steady. Margie saw a

"dark room with a faint glimmer of light. The image becomes slightly brighter and the light is revealed as a candle burning. It is a room with a fireplace and an overstuffed sofa with large, comfortable-looking pillows. The candle is slowly getting brighter. The fireplace looks warm and inviting (although not lit). The couch looks comfortable and safe and warm. The walls have tapestries and the room is full of different textures. However, there are no windows or plants or any living things. There is no sunlight. I have to put in windows (to see out and be seen) and many plants so the sunlight will stream in and give the room an energy and life that have been missing. The fireplace should be lit and the candle allowed to burn out naturally. I feel that in spite of fears and anxieties I do have hope."

The changes Margie wanted to make in her room give glimpses into some of the changes she needs to make in her life.

Symbolism is a very personal matter. It is not uncommon to open the "Body Room" door and see parts of the body. Occasionally we choose very literal images. But although they are literal, their meaning varies with the individual. The body parts that Beth saw represented a traumatic experience she had during surgery. She was no longer able to feel the integrity of her body. Vicki, who works in an auto parts store, saw her body parts neatly lined up on shelves. For her this symbolized the way she saw her body as a commodity.

A window is not necessarily a window. For Margie, a window was a way of making contact with the outside world and of bringing in energy. Windows can also be ways of shedding light (awareness) on the darkness. Joanne had a room where the window had no glass. She felt overwhelmed by stimuli from the outside.

Please find the meaning of your symbols by asking them to speak. You and only you know why you choose certain images, and what they are trying to tell you about yourself. Sometimes these messages are vague, requiring persistence in order to understand them. It is sometimes helpful to take some extra time and engage your images in dialogue to try to bring out more information. Your persistence will reward you with valuable material that might take years to find on an analyst's couch.

VI
CULTURAL ROOTS

Your body image has been formed out of every experience you have ever had: the way your parents related to and touched your body as a baby and a growing child; what you have learned from your role models about what it is like to live in and value a body; the acceptance and rejection you have felt from your peers; every negative and positive piece of feedback you and your body have ever received from people whose opinions count to you; and the ways you have perceived your body to fit or not fit the cultural image.

Each of us has both familial and cultural roots which interact to shape us into the people we are. The culture in which we live has shaped our parents' values which in turn influenced the choices they made in childrearing which in turn effect the values we develop. On the other hand, those features in our upbringing that were unique to our particular families created in each of us a ready and fertile soil for some cultural seeds to flourish. It is not possible to understand how we have arrived at the relationship we have with our bodies without also understanding the culture in which we have developed.

We live in a culture that places a very high premium on physical appearance. If this is true for the culture as a whole, it is doubly true for women who have been brought up believing that their chief, perhaps their only role in life, is as ornament, wife, and mother. Although the Women's Movement has made strides in broadening the choices available, the majority of women today still believe they must be attractive enough to snare a man who will provide the ticket for the unfolding of their biological and social destiny. Conforming to the current image of beauty guarantees fulfillment and seals a woman's fate. For most of us the myth dies hard.

Men in our culture are traditionally raised to be powerful, physically agile, and successful. The male self-image hinges primarily on how well he measures up to these requirements. While some men especially when young worry over the size of their genitals and their physical strength, the concern about body adequacy is finally less important than success in the world. With other ways of validating themselves, men can maintain their self image intact even in the face of serious physical flaws. The quest for physical perfection remains woman's domain.

What is beauty? How do we know if we are attractive? Somewhere there is an ideal image which women use as a yardstick. We live in a time when for the first time in human history the media are powerful forces in shaping our thoughts, values, ideals, and aspirations. Although films and fashion magazines have been influencing the cultural norm for many years, it is only since television that the media have gained the power to manipulate our lives. The majority of people in our society under the age of 35 have been raised by TV, the electronic babysitter, and much of what we believe and have come to know about the world we have learned from this surrogate parent.

Today's woman is constantly told by media images how she measures up or fails to measure up to the unreal, restrictive, elusive, and ephemeral esthetic standard. And as Deborah Hutton said in *Vogue Complete Beauty,* "The greatest misfortune [is] to be born out of one's era, with features appropriate for some undiscovered style, but hopelessly inappropriate for the one of the day."

The media communicates its messages through images which tyrannize our fleshy, flawed, embodied realities. No matter how much we try to control or diet or deodorize our bodies, we cannot hope to match the illusion on the screen or the printed page.

As women, we are especially vulnerable to the media message. We are rewarded for directing our attention toward others and for looking outside ourselves for guidance. We are encouraged to be passive and receptive. We tend to look to others for cues about who we are, what we should be, and how we should value ourselves. First it was our parents, then our peers, then our partners, and then most pervasively the media.

•

Stop a moment and reflect on what your ideal of female beauty is. What image are you carrying around in your mind's eye? See if you can discover where your ideal came from. Consider how you measure up to it, and whether it is even remotely within your grasp to measure up to it, given your natural resources.

•

Our culture has an obsession with thinness. Fat is seen as Public Enemy Number One and dieting has become the national way of life. It has not always been this way. Throughout most of our history, an extra padding of flesh has always had both survival and esthetic values for women. In those days thinness in women was considered an aberration to be pitied. What has happened to change this?

The shift can be traced back to the 1920s. Those were the days of the flapper, the beginning of women's emancipation, when the emerging desire for equality with men manifested itself in a change in clothing and in bodies. Gone was the accentuation of curves. Gone was the extra padding. Gone in fact was anything that advertised a woman's womanliness. Breast, hips, curves, and flesh came to be seen as impediments to equality with men, to be done away with or at least hidden.

Physicians also have promoted thinness as a way to health. In 1959 a major medical study advocated a major downward adjustment of the height-weight table. People of normal weight woke up to discover that they had been declared overweight by ten to fifteen pounds practically overnight! As a result, a national mania for thinness sprang up, bringing with it a giant diet and fitness industry. A new breed of women was born whose major career was to lose that last ten to fifteen pounds.

Surely the trend toward health and fitness has had many positive consequences, encouraging people to eat healthier foods and to exercise more. However, a new kind of tyranny has emerged, to be eternally young, fit, and lean whatever the price.

Caught between equally powerful media messages at one moment extolling the virtues of slenderness and at the next tempting us with images of forbidden morsels, we are locked in a double bind. Damned if we do and damned if we don't. And the bulimic who gorges herself to the point of bursting and then sticks her finger down her throat to eliminate the traces of her excesses is a living manifestation of this bind. Bulimia is an ingenious, albeit dangerous and painful, solution to an impossible dilemma. Is it any wonder that our bodies have become the battlefield for our conflicting drives?

Data from several recent medical studies conflict with the finding of the 1959 study. They suggest that some extra flesh can actually extend life and improve health and resistance to disease. Whether it is healthier to be plump or to be lean, it is probably more dangerous to our health to yo-yo up and down in weight than to remain stably overweight.

We must begin to question some of the notions about weight and health that have shaped cultural values and have pressured many of us into going against the dictates of our bodies. We must also begin to question where to draw the line between what is normal and what is overweight. The height-weight tables have recently returned to their pre-1959 level, thereby sanctioning at least medically the return of a healthy coating of flesh to the body. How long it will take to reverse the general insanity about weight remains to be seen.

Feminism has helped to change our cultural values over the last twenty years. The challenging voice of the Women's Movement tells us not to minimize ourselves, but to be more, to be larger, to be more powerful, to expand our horizons. However, for some women this opportunity is felt as pressure, bringing with it a new sense of inadequacy. They must perform in a realm for which they have been ill-prepared. And since a woman's sense of adequacy or inadequacy often translates into the adequacy or inadequacy of her body, it is the body that is often blamed for her success or failure. For other women, the move out into the world of competition with men is often experienced as a threat both to men and to the women themselves. If a woman becomes too powerful she fears alienating people and finding herself alone. It is my sense that women respond to some internal (and externally-supported) quota about how much space they are allowed to take up. The more power a woman is permitted, the more she is required (by herself and society) to make her body smaller, less important, less threatening.

Living in a time of rapidly changing roles and contradictory and confusing demands — eat/don't eat; be more/be less — it should come as little surprise that woman's body has become a confused battlefield rather than a home. Enlightened feminism has not guaranteed immunity to this mind-body malaise.

It is necessary to dredge up the past so that we can understand the influences at work in us. If we know what excess baggage we are carrying and even where we picked that baggage up, we are in a better position to let the baggage go and move on with our lives.

VII

MUCKRAKING

Our families act as agents and mouthpieces for spreading cultural values. They raise and socialize us according to prevailing standards, but each family has its own special handwriting that makes each of our histories unique. What we learn from our families sets the stage for further learning about ourselves. If our families have given us a positive sense of our bodies and our selves either through their own example or through their behavior toward us, we will be more receptive to similar messages from the outside world. Similarly, if we have learned to experience ourselves negatively in the family, we will be rich and receptive soil in which the negative seeds of cultural values can take root. We will tend to process any information from the outside through selective filters that support what we already "know" about ourselves, and to reject any messages that conflict with that "knowledge."

The following exercises deal with material of a very sensitive nature. You will uncover memories of important people and incidents that have played a powerful role in the development of your body image.

As you undoubtedly know, your relationship with your body is an emotionally loaded subject. Some of the material you uncover may be difficult or painful. If you experience discomfort, I want to encourage you to keep looking at this material. Your subconscious mind will present you only with images and memories that *you are ready to see* and deal with.

Trust yourself and your own process and remember that whatever you uncover in any of these exercises you have *survived already*. It is time to reexperience these memories so that you can *learn* from them and *deal* with them using all your resources. If at any time the going gets too rough, you can choose to step away from the material and open your eyes until you feel ready to go back inside to do some more work.

I want to encourage you not to be afraid of the feelings that come up. The more feeling you bring to your imaginal work, the more powerful it will be in transforming you. Feelings are natural and healthy. They are your system's way of expressing and cleansing itself of old baggage that it is time for you to discard.

Since this chapter and parts of the next are designed to bring old material to the surface, your daily life and perhaps even your dreams will be affected. This is natural. There comes a point in any healing process where you will be painfully aware of your issues and yet still lack the tools for change. Be kind to yourself and be patient. Please do not skip over this very important phase of the work. If you do, you will be denying yourself an opportunity to clear the way for the kind of change that motivated you to pick up this book in the first place.

EXERCISE 8
Rolling Back the Years

1. Sit comfortably, close your eyes and relax.
2. Imagine that you are moving back in time rapidly back through the years as if each year of your life were a card in a Rolodex file. . . growing younger and younger until you stop at some point when you were a small baby. . .
3. How old are you? Look around and notice what is around you. Are you alone? If not, who is there with you? Are you feeling safe and comfortable, or do you feel vulnerable in some way? Notice what it's like to have this baby's body. Take a few minutes to experience the world through fresh and innocent eyes. . .
4. Imagine that time is beginning to move forward now. *Feel* your body growing, becoming fuller and larger and more competent as you move into childhood. At some point stop the action. . .
5. How old are you? Look down at your child's body. How do you feel in and about this body? What do you like about it? What do you not like? Move around and experience the quality of your movement and energy. . . How are you feeling in relation to the world?
6. Time is beginning to move forward now, but more slowly than before. See if you can trace the changes occurring in your body as you begin to approach puberty, letting yourself *feel* how your body is

changing and developing and in what stages. . . Notice how you are feeling about the process happening to your body. . . Move around in this body and notice how that feels. . . Become aware of how you are feeling in your adolescent body in relation to the world. . . In reaching this stage what part of childhood must you let go of and what part of adulthood must you now adopt?

7. Time is beginning to move forward again. *Feel* yourself leaving your adolescent self behind as you mature gradually into the body you now have. Take as much time as you need to let that process unfold in detail, noticing whatever changes in shape and size that your body has gone through to reach its present state. Notice what you leave behind and what you take with you into adulthood. . . Notice and experience any shifts in your feelings about your body as you gradually move into the body you have now. . .

8. Rest. Notice how it feels to be back in your present body after your journey through the years. Open your eyes when you are ready.

Worksheet

1. Describe your experience of being a baby as if it were happening right now.
2. Describe your experience of being a child as if it were happening right now.
3. Describe the process of maturing from childhood to adolescence including feelings, gains, losses, etc.
4. Describe your experience of being in an adolescent body as if it were happening right now.
5. Describe the changes your body and body image have gone through since adolescence.
6. Can you pinpoint the period in your life when you began to feel negative about your body? Describe the circumstances surrounding this shift.
7. What of importance have you learned from this exercise?
8. Indicate any difficulties you had in doing the exercise.
10. Comments.

Guiding Words

By slowing down the action and following our development it becomes possible to identify milestones where there have been significant shifts in our body attitudes. We can begin to look more closely at those turning points for information about how we lost our way. What happened? Why did our bodies become a prison rather than a home for us? When we locate the injuries we can be more accurate in directing the healing process.

For some of you perhaps the disturbance came early. Maybe when you look back on your life you will find no period when you felt at home in your body. In some families babies and young children go hungry for the comfort of touch. Early touch is very important for letting us know on a very basic level that we (and our bodies) are acceptable and lovable. The quality of that touch can communicate love and valuing or duty and devaluing. Our young bodies take in those messages, whatever they are, without the judgment necessary to put them in perspective. We simply feel and learn about ourselves and about life through these feelings.

Most of you will probably discover puberty or pre-puberty as the period in your life when your attitude toward your body went amiss. In general, those are times of intense feelings of bodily awkwardness. It is during adolescence that we begin to measure ourselves against our peers. It is a time when acceptance is most important. Do I fit in? Am I sexually attractive? What do I do with my sexual feelings? Will my peers like me? Am I O.K.?

The rapid changes that occur in our bodies during this period are stressful and often result in a confused body image even if everything in our environment is positive (an impossibility, of course). Many of us suffer loss as our fathers retreat from our budding sexuality because of their own discomfort; other young girls receive more sexual attention from their fathers and other males than they can handle. Perhaps our mothers begin to experience us as rivals, or equally detrimental, as extensions and reflections of themselves. Many girls manifest their conflicts about growing up by gaining weight, or by dieting themselves into anorexia. Both approaches have the effect of hiding the telltale signs of developing womanhood.

What we learn about ourselves and our bodies during adolescence often becomes engraved into our body images and carried over into later life.

•

Reflect on whether and how that has happened to you.

EXERCISE 9
Family Portrait

This exercise will be most enlightening if you rely on the fresh vision of your imaginal eyes for information rather than drawing from what you already think you know about your family. In order to ease memory, *Worksheet* questions are interwoven with the exercise.

1. Sit comfortably, close your eyes and relax.
2. In your imagination, go back into your past to a time when you were much younger—to a formative and impressionable time as a child or early adolescent. Create an opportunity to bring together many members of your family in one place. (Perhaps it will be a gathering that actually happened.) Include any relatives or people who were important to you in your early years.
3. Gather everyone together—including yourself—as if you were posing for a family portrait. . . Notice who is present. . . And who is missing. . . Notice how you are arranged and where you are in relation to others. . . How old are you?
4. Now step out of the picture with your consciousness, leaving your body just where it is.
5. Notice their characteristic postures. What messages—both positive and negative—are they communicating to the world with their bodies?. . .

Worksheet

1. Who is present in your portrait and how old were you at the time?
2. What were the non-verbal messages communicated to you and to the world by their bodies?
3. As role models, how have they taught you to feel about your body?

•

6. Return to your imagination. Now separate out the males as a group. Are they attractive? How are they "masculine" and "male"? How do they appear to relate to their own bodies and their sexuality?. . . Walk up to them and sense how you feel in their presence. . . What have they taught you about what it means to be a female?

Worksheet

1. What was there to learn about maleness from the males in your family?
2. What did you learn about being a woman from your experiences with these males?

•

7. Return to your imagination and, keeping your consciousness outside the image, separate out the females in your family as a group, including yourself. . . How do you feel about their bodies when you look at them?. . . Notice their body types. . . The way they carry and dress their bodies. . . How does your body measure up in comparison to their bodies?. . . What can you tell from looking at them about their feelings about their own bodies?. . . What have you learned from them about how to value and care for your own body?
8. How do they feel about being women?. . . What do they teach you about what a woman is? Or is not?. . . What can you tell about their attitudes toward their own sexuality?. . . In what ways do they project it?. . . And in what ways do they mask it?. . .

Worksheet

1. How would you characterize the women in your family as a group in regard to appearance, self presentation, and ease in their bodies?
2. Do they seem to value their bodies? How do they take care of their bodies?
3. What did you learn from them about sexuality?
4. What did these women teach you about how to feel about your own body?
5. Which women have been important role models?

•

9. Return to your imagination. Reassemble your whole family in one place. As you look at these people, what feelings come up for you?. . .

Worksheet

1. What feelings come up for you as you contemplate your family as a group?. . .
2. How have you incorporated your family into your body image?
3. Of what you have taken in, what do you wish to keep? What do you wish to discard?
4. To attain the body image you want for yourself, what kind of role model would have been helpful that was unavailable in your family?
5. Comments.

Guiding Words

One of the most important ways that our families can influence our body image is through their own body images. Our families are our primary teachers during our formative years. What they teach us by example serves as the basis for what we learn subsequently. If our parents or other significant family members negate, deny, or otherwise devalue their *own* bodies, we pick up this negative judgment from them and apply it to our own bodies.

It can be a very subtle and even insidious way of learning since it comes through non-verbal channels such as body language and behavior. It can slip into our attitudes toward the world so quietly that we may not be conscious that we have adopted our family's viewpoint.

Doing *Family Portrait* is one way to tap into information about your role models and what you have most likely internalized from them into your own body image. Another way to ferret out this information is to look through your family photo album and study what their body language—posture, expressions, clothing, relative positions—reveals to you. You can apply this same exercise to your real, in-the-flesh relatives who will unwittingly provide you with a wealth of information.

When Joan looked at her imaginal family she saw

> "people with no bodies, just heads. They show no physical expression. Nobody is touching. They are devoid of affection and devoid of life. There seems to be a family standard to ignore the body. They taught me nothing—except to deny my body. I have learned to repress my sexuality and to be disconnected from it."

The women in Donna's family were all overweight and appeared ashamed of their bodies.

> "They were basically hiding their womanliness and denying their sexuality as if it wasn't okay to be a woman. They taught me that if I didn't watch out, my body would spread and I'd have a weight problem. They taught me my body was to be hidden away or dieted away. They taught me to ignore my body, to pay attention to it only when it got sick—that was the only time."

Donna has had a steady stream of minor health complaints all her life. It is one of the few times she acknowledges her body. The other times come with weight gain. She lives in dread of becoming fat and has been anorexic and overweight at different times in her life. Much of the disgust she has toward her body is focused on those areas that declare her womanliness—her breasts, hips, buttocks, and thighs.

EXERCISE 10
Parental Images

Please do this exercise at least two times, once in an imagined scene with your mother and on a separate occasion with your father. You can also do the exercise with other people who were influential in your early years.

Part 1

1. Sit comfortably, close your eyes and relax.
2. Go back to a time in your life when you were young, either a child or an adolescent. Picture a familiar situation involving you and your mother or father. . . How old are you? What are you doing together?. . .

3. Look at this person and observe how you feel. . . Pay attention to any feelings or associations attached to this image. . .

4. Scan the image as if it were right in front of you; look at this person closely, noticing the details of face, body, expressions, gestures, carriage, clothes, and grooming. . .

5. What can you gather from non-verbal cues about this person's feelings about her/his own body and sexuality?

6. What do you like or dislike about this person's body?. . . What awarenesses come up for you?. . . Are your bodies alike or different? How?

7. Imagine merging with this other body and then separating. . . Which is easier for you?. . .

8. Move closer to this person, and observe carefully how you feel about your body in her/his presence? How do you feel about yourself? Do you feel accepted by this person?

9. Ask this person if she/he accepts and loves you and your body. . . What is missing for you in her/his response?

10. What do you feel that you need from this person right now? Can you ask for it?. . . What response do you get?

11. Reach out to touch this person. . . How do you feel about doing this?. . . How does this person respond?. . . Does she/he touch you back? What does the content or quality of the response communicate to you about your body and your self?. . .

12. What do you want or need to express or communicate right now to this person? Take a moment to find in yourself the feelings and words that demand expression right now. . .

13. Look at this person directly in the eye and express whatever you want to say with feeling and conviction. . .

Worksheet

1. Describe your experience with this parent in the present tense using as much detail as you can recall:

2. What sort of example did this person set for you? What do you wish to keep from what you learned from this person? What do you wish to discard?

3. What was her/his behavior toward you?

4. What do you need to express to this parent (either from the past or the present)? Is this something you are actually willing to do with your parent?

5. What is positive in your interaction with this parent?

6. Take some time to imagine what the child in you really needed from this parental figure so that your body image could have been more positive. From this information (and from question No. 5), create for yourself a *Positive Parent Image.* Consider some of the following:
   - What would you have needed in the way of nurturing (feeding of food, love, support and affirmation)?
   - How would you have wished this parent to express love for you? In words, touch, actions, etc.?
   - How would you have needed this parent to deal with your aggression and sexuality?
   - How would you have needed this parent to relate to your needs for closeness and bonding while at the same time allowing your autonomy and separateness?
   - What qualities would you like this parent to have modeled for you?

7. What is negative in your interaction with this parent? From this information create for yourself a *Negative Parent Image* which you will use in Part 2.

8. Comments.

Part 2

1. Sit comfortably, close your eyes and relax.

2. Imagine that you are standing. In front and to the left of you is your *Negative Parent Image.* In front and to the right is your *Positive Parent Image.*

3. Turn toward your *Positive Parent Image* and see how much you can open yourself to the flow of positive feelings available to you from this parent. . . Let yourself receive all the affirming, nurturing, supportive feelings coming from this parent to you, allowing yourself to bathe in the love coming from this parent to you. . .

4. Notice what you can let in. . . Notice what you are blocking out. . . Notice *how* you are blocking it out. . .

5. Examine your resistance and ask yourself: What would be the risk of letting these feelings in? What would you stand to lose?

6. Now turn toward your *Negative Parent Image* and express whatever feelings you have toward that person that may be contributing to your resistance.

7. Turn once again toward your *Positive Parent Image* and repeat Steps Nos. 3 and 4.

8. Move back and forth between these two *Parent Images* until you can clear a path for taking in positive feelings or at least recognize the *clean up* work that you need to do with your *Negative Parent Figure* and the *opening up* work that you need to do in yourself. Take as much time as you need to do this work.

Worksheet

1. What is blocking your ability or willingness to accept positive feelings or information from your *Positive Parent Image?*

2. What work remains for you to do with your parents either in fantasy or in the flesh in order to improve your relationship to your body?

3. Comments.

Guiding Words

It is completely natural for us as young people to *identify* with our parents. As women, it is our mothers with whom our identification is the strongest. Many of us have been fed prophecies such as "You're going to grow up and look just like your mother!" Many of us grow up identified with our mothers. For some of us it is nearly impossible to see ourselves and our bodies in their own right as separate from our mothers'. Such was the case for Eve, a very thin woman with a fat mother and a fat body image.

> "On the beach with my mother, we are both lying on towels reading. I'm sixteen and wearing a two-piece bathing suit. I'm annoyed because she's wearing one too. I think I'm more than annoyed, I'm angry at her, and embarrassed to be near her because she looks so fat and I'm afraid of how she will reflect on me. She doesn't seem to be self-conscious. How she looked bothered me, made me concerned about how I would develop. I worried a lot about it then and I worry now."

Sometimes it is not your mother's body but what it represents that provokes an identification or in some cases a dis-identification. In her work with *Family Portrait* and *Parental Images,* Joanne came to some stunning realizations. She did *Parental Images* with her real mother and with her grandmother who had raised her. Her mother is fat and her major memories of her were warm and loving and revolved around food. For Joanne, *love* came to equal *fat*. Her grandmother, on the other hand, was a thin woman who could not provide her with emotional warmth and physical contact.

> "She never accepted me. She was critical and unbending. Her body was controlled and not very playful. I hate control, I am out of control concerning my body and what I put into it. Her body taught stiffness and control. . . I rebelled against my grandmother, saying, 'If you are in control then I am out of control.' That is exactly how I've been around food issues. When I go to my grandmother's house it's uncomfortable because if I ask for seconds she calls me a 'little pig' so I sneak food there. I feel shameful and deceitful."

Joanne's body has played out her conflicting internal images by alternately being anorexic, bulimic, and overweight.

It is common for a mother to see her daughter as an extension and reflection of herself. When she is overinvested in her daughter's bodily life, she lives vicariously through her daughter and must manage her eating and dressing habits as well as her behavior. This makes it very difficult for the daughter to feel ownership of her own body and to create an identity for herself separate from her mother.

Especially as puberty approaches, competition with our mothers and other close female models can effect body image. Julia's mother felt that she was no longer beautiful and unconsciously saw in her daughter a threat to her own self-esteem. She gave her daughter a fear of her own power and a sense of inadequacy about her body. For Bea it was her fraternal twin sister who was her major rival for parental attention. Although Bea was considered the brighter of the two, it was her sister who turned everyone's eye with her exceptional good looks. Bea had grown up with great insecurity about her own appearance. She has tenaciously clung to her "knowledge" that she is plain and always second best.

While our fathers are considerably less important to us as body role models, as the first significant male in our lives, they can have a powerful impact on how we adapt to our womanliness. Puberty often marks a shift in the father-daughter relationship. In Virginia's case, her father's own discomfort with his daughter's emerging sexuality manifested itself as a withdrawal of affection.

> "I had been Daddy's little girl. Father and I had been very close, but as I developed he pulled away and didn't know how to relate to me. I was

saddened by the loss and nurtured myself with food. Maybe even my period was slow in coming as a reaction to my fear of growing up."

Some fathers cross the line into incest, leaving traces of shame on our body images. Whether our fathers react to our burgeoning womanhood with abandonment or invasion, the lesson is that it is not safe or acceptable to be pretty and sexual.

We tend to *internalize* parental treatment (positive, critical, invasive, or denying) in a do-unto-myself-as-I-have-been-done-to manner. If you have swallowed your critical parent whole you will continue the criticism on your own.

Hopefully you were able to tap into some very important information about the source of your difficulties with your body. However, discovering what was negative or missing in your relationship with your parents does not constitute a license for open hunting. Blaming your parents for what is wrong with the way you relate to your body will not solve anything. What *will* help is understanding the roots of your attitudes and behavior so that you can begin to change.

You can also use *Parental Images* to observe your relationship with your parents in the present. You can do this simply by altering Step No. 2 of the exercise and choosing a present-day context. You may want to confront your parents in the flesh.

Most of you will begin the process of identifying what you want to discard in your body image and what you want to keep in order to make a clear statement to yourself and to the world about who *you* are as a separate individual apart from your parents.

We can find new role models for ourselves that fit our mature aspirations. We can use our imagination as a place of healing where we can give ourselves the kinds of strokes and affirmations that were not available in our real families. One way to do this is to create a regular meditation based on your interactions with your *Positive Parent Image.* This will not only help you to heal some of your old wounds and fill in the missing pieces, but will also help you to become more receptive in general to positive feedback that is available in your world.

VIII
WHO'S WRONG WITH YOUR BODY IMAGE?

This chapter and the next represent a transitional phase of *Transforming Body Image.* We will be doing a combination of three kinds of work: 1) Clarifying what you are carrying around as excess baggage; 2) Identifying some of the obstacles that block your path; and 3) Beginning to discard the baggage.

Excess baggage is any knowledge, belief, or feeling that does not really belong to you or no longer serves you. In the case of your body image, it consists of everything you have swallowed whole from your culture, your family, and other people. When you take in information or feedback from the outside and swallow it whole, you have never really evaluated it to see whether it should become part of you. Since we have been socialized to look outside of ourselves for everything, we easily adopt other people's attitudes that really are not relevant to us or sometimes endanger us.

Seed Questions

1. Make a list of the people in your life who have had a major impact on the development of your body image. These should be people in your past and present whose values have shaped your attitudes toward yourself.

EXERCISE 11
Imaginary Visitors

1. Sit comfortably, close your eyes and relax.
2. Take a few minutes to get in touch with how you see yourself, how

you feel in and about your body, and how you talk to yourself about your body—right now. . .

3. Carry out the instructions in this step with each of the people on your list, one at a time, spending as much time with each as it takes to ferret out the needed information.

- Imagine yourself standing naked.
- Imagine that this person enters the room and walks around you, looking at you from all angles.
- Carefully observe your feelings.
- Imagine what this person is noticing and thinking about your body.
- Ask this person to tell you what she/he is seeing.
- Get in touch with your body image again and notice whether and how it has been influenced by this visitor, both in this exercise and in your development.
- See if you have anything to say to this person right now. Say it with feeling and conviction.
- Stop and write down what you have taken into your body image from this person that you wish to discard.

4. Scan your body now to see where your perceptions have been influenced by others. . . For every negative judgment that you have swallowed, balance it with *two* positive statements about this part of your body. . . Take as much time as you need.

5. Study your list of excess baggage. Imagine that each observation or judgment is "food for thought." Put each bit of this food in your mouth, experience how it tastes. . . Chew it, see if you want to swallow it and make it a part of you, or see if you want to spit it out. . . Vividly imagine yourself swallowing it or spitting it out, being clear with yourself about what you are choosing to discard or to make a part of you. . . Take as much time as you need.

Worksheet

1. Think back to the positive feedback you received. How much of it are you willing to let in? How and why do you resist letting it in?
2. How have you tried to change yourself to please each person?
3. Which pieces of excess baggage seem easy to let go of?
4. Which are you unable or unwilling to let go of?
5. What would be the risk or cost to you of letting it go?
6. Comments.

Guiding Words

Hopefully, you are beginning to see the origins of some of the chronic and habitual ways you see, feel, and talk to your body. By identifying and sorting out each judgment, you begin to see that you have a choice about whether to accept it or not.

When Sharon invited her mother in:

> "Her judgments are rattled off at almost every body part. They are very familiar and powerful. 'I'm never good enough.' . . . Mother's judgments have been important ones that have stuck. I am attached to them. They keep me from enjoying myself sexually."

When Brenda did the exercise with her aunt she discovered that she associated her aunt's flamboyant, passionate, body-oriented nature with emotional instability and suffering. Her mother, on the contrary, was subdued, in control, and out of touch with her body. . . "Perhaps I'm afraid if I do become more affirming of my own body, I will be unstable and reckless like her."

All of us are bound and attached to other people by powerful feelings, positive or negative. Most of the time our feelings toward others are a blend of positive and negative. It is easy to harbor negative feelings toward someone who has hurt us. These feelings weigh us down with excess baggage and leave us vulnerable.

We cannot control everything that happens to us, but we can control how we react. We can choose to nurse our wounds and feel sorry for ourselves, spinning our wheels. Or we can choose to let go of our pain and move on with our lives.

Seed Questions

1. Think of the people in your life who have left a negative mark on your body image (*e.g.,* Mother, Slim and Perfect Aunt Josephine, the boys in your 8th grade class, etc.).
2. Arrange them in order beginning with the person who did the greatest damage to the way you feel about your body.

EXERCISE 12
Wheel of Chains

1. Sit comfortably, close your eyes and relax.

2. Experience yourself sitting quietly in a large, sun-filled space, either outdoors or indoors. . . Feel the warmth and radiance of the sun. . .

3. Mentally invite into your space those people from your past and present who have taught you to negate your own beauty. Watch them as they enter, noticing that each one is carrying a heavy chain with a loop on one end. Invite them to sit in a circle with you in the center. . .

4. When they all sit down, let yourself experience your feelings as you sit surrounded by these people. . .

5. One at a time, deal with each person in your circle according to the order you chose above.

6. See this person standing up and walking over to you. Take the looped end of the chain in your hand and place it around your body. As you do this, acknowledge that it is *you* who are binding this person to you with a chain that represents some negativity. . . Watch this person return to you with a chain that represents some negativity. . . Watch this person return again to the circle.

7. Sit quietly and let yourself remember the feelings that bind you to this person. . .

8. Turn and face the person, take a moment to gather your thoughts and then express them as clearly as you can with all the emotion that fits your words. (Remember the more feeling you can bring to the image the more healing it is.)

9. Give this person the chance to respond.

10. Thank the person.

11. Repeat Steps Nos. 6-9 with each person in your circle.

12. Look around the circle once more and check if there are any left-over negative feelings that you haven't expressed to your satisfaction. If you find any, express them now. . .

13. You are in the center of this circle bound to all of these people by chains that represent bonds of negative feelings such as pain, anger, shame, envy, and hate. Experience with all your senses the heaviness

and limitation of this kind of bondage. . . Ask yourself: "Do I want to remain bound, or do I want to let go?

14. If you wish to remain bound, acknowledge this as a decision. Stop here and pledge that you will examine this decision. If you choose to release yourself from the confines of this negativity, go on with the exercise.

15. Return to the circle. Experience yourself in the center of a ray of sunshine. . . Feel the intensity of its golden warmth melting any traces of pain in you. . . Imagine a column of light filling the interior of your body, and with each breath you take, breathe in a warmth that nurtures you and allows that inner core to grow brighter and stronger. . . With each breath allow your heart to open and your generosity of spirit to grow. . . Really *feel* your warmth and radiance. . . Take several minutes.

16. As your inner strength grows, you can allow the openness of your heart to manifest itself as feelings of forgiveness. . . Concentrate your attention on opening your heart, on letting go more and more of the negativity that binds you to these people. . .

17. Do this step for each person in your circle. Gaze at the person and as you do, breathe deeply and *feel* your inner warmth and strength increase as you direct forgiveness to this person. . . Concentrating on the feelings in your heart, say the words, "I forgive you, _____." Say it again and use the warmth in you to melt the chain that joins you, watching it transform into a delicate golden thread linking you in spirit. . .

18. Now look around you at the faces in your circle, at the glistening golden threads that join you to these people through heart and spirit instead of pain and resentment. *Feel* what this is like for you. . .

19. Turn your attention now to opening your heart to yourself, enveloping yourself in forgiveness for all the ways that you have disappointed yourself, past and the present. . . Say these words to yourself with feeling:

"May I be happy. . . May I be free from tension, fear, worry, hate and suffering. . . May I let go of all things that bind me to pain and cause me suffering. . . May I be whole. . . May I experience my own grace. . . May I be at peace."

20. Stay quietly with these feelings as long as you can permit yourself and then gently open your eyes.

Worksheet

For each person in your circle please ask yourself:
1. How did this person cause you pain?
2. In what way(s) did this person's behavior affect your relationship to your body?
3. What feelings and statements did you need to express to this person?
4. Are you willing to let go of your grievances against this person? If not, what do you gain or accomplish for yourself by holding on to your grievances?
5. Who in your circle remains unforgiven? Are you willing to keep trying until you can dissolve the bondage? If not, why not?

Guiding Words

Joanne invited into her circle "old boyfriends, people who raped me, my father, my grandmother, lots of men, and two women I am jealous of."

> "I hate the chains. I want to break loose. I like letting out the anger and fear I've felt all these years. Some of these people go back 17 years. I can transform the chains and understand that these people are victims too. I can forgive them. The hardest one to forgive is a man who raped me when I was thirteen. I feel so much anger, but he was young then. . . I pray he has changed. The golden threads are beautiful. I wanted to bury all those people, but forgiveness feels better."

It is important to confront and express our negative feelings before we can let them go. We don't often have the opportunity to express what is in our hearts either because the risk is too great or simply because those people who have hurt us are no longer active in our lives. By using our imagination and having fantasy dialogues with them (especially when we put feeling and conviction into our words) we can safely release a great deal of emotional toxicity from our systems. An imaginary confrontation can act as a safe substitute for the real thing or can serve as a rehearsal for a real interaction.

Some of you may find that certain people in your life are difficult or impossible to forgive at first. If this happens, please do this exercise again, concentrating on that person only. You may find that you need to spend more time on the step in the exercise where you express your feelings to that person. If you have the opportunity and the risk does not feel too overwhelming, why not confront this person in the flesh, or spend some time writing about the feelings that are keeping you stuck, or writing a letter to this person that you do not send. Please make a pledge to keep working at the problem until it becomes easier to let go of these chains that bind you.

I suggested to Joanne that she do the exercise again, this time concentrating on forgiving herself. This was her experience.

> "My chains were of self-loathing and self-deprecation. I became full of glowing energy—a glowing orb of light. I said 'I forgive myself for all the pain I've caused myself.' And my other self became a glowing energy too. I was crying. I feel good that I could forgive myself and transform the chain. I feel like I have a twin that has known me all along who probably was very perplexed that I put myself through all the torture and self-destructive behavior."

When Francine did *Chains* with her mother, she got in touch with the "stubborn little girl" who was convinced that her mother hurt her on purpose because she did not love her. She found that she still wanted to nurse that hurt, because she was not yet ready to take responsibility for her own life. Because she holds on so stubbornly, she is locked in battle with her mother. Her inability to forgive her mother saddened Francine and spurred her on until she was finally successful and forgave her mother.

Forgiving those who have wronged us is not easy work, but it is crucial if we are to move on with our lives. Most of us perversely would rather hold on to our pain than let it go. We can then feel sorry for ourselves and blame all of our suffering on others. Some people live with the mistaken notion that they *are* their pain, that without it they would no longer be special. It's true that letting go of our grievances leaves a vacuum which can sometimes be perceived as a loss or a sense of emptiness. Perhaps it would help to look at this analogy. When you clean out your closet you throw away things that hold memories, but you are making room for a new wardrobe. In your emotional housecleaning you are creating a very special and fertile kind of emptiness, a fertile void, that should be embraced as an essential part of making room for new growth.

We often think that to forgive means giving up some piece of our self-respect, that somehow we lose face. This is what our pride and stubbornness tell us. Nothing could be further from the truth. In fact, it requires inner *strength,* not weakness, to forgive those who have wronged us and to move on with our lives. We lose nothing but our chains.

IX
HOLDING ON
TO WHAT?

For many of us a negative body attitude serves a defensive function: It maintains the status quo. It protects us against feeling, doing, or being something that we perceive as risky. Very often we are busy protecting ourselves from risks or losses that threatened us in the past, but are in no way dangerous to us now. Often we use our negative body attitudes so that we do not have to take responsibility for our lives as adults.

In this chapter and the next, you will begin to look at your resistance to change, the ways you are limiting yourself, and how these limitations serve you. When you have identified the function your negative attitude performs, you can begin to look around for other ways of fulfilling that function. Perhaps you will discover that many of these mechanisms do not serve you at all and you can choose to let them go.

In order to let go of these mechanisms, you will first have to identify them. Choosing to let go of these mechanisms requires a *you* who is willing to make such a choice, a *you* who, from the center of your being, chooses a life of wholeness and health.

EXERCISE 13
Cloaks of Identity*

1. Write down ten words or phrases that describe your negative feelings and attitudes about your body, *e.g.,* "I am fat," "I am ungainly," etc.
2. Choose the five that you feel closest to and write each of these on a small piece of paper.

* Adapted from Frances E. Vaughan's *Awakening Intuition*. New York: Anchor, 1979.

3. Arrange these pieces of paper in a stack with the ones that feel most essential to you on the bottom and the ones that are least essential on the top.

4. Sit comfortably with your stack of papers within easy reach. Close your eyes and relax.

5. (Please follow this two step procedure with each piece of paper.) Pick up the first piece of paper and look at the words which define your relationship to your body. Allow yourself to *experience fully* what it means to you and your life to identify yourself this way.

— How does it feel to be defined by this?

— Be aware of all the sensations, thoughts, feelings that go along with this definition of yourself.

— Acknowledge and experience in fantasy the many ramifications of this self-definition in your life (relationships, career, self-image, health, etc.).

— Experience the way in which it limits you and also the things it gives you permission to be or do.

When you have fully experienced this piece of paper turn it over and as you do imagine that you are letting go of this self identification as if you were taking off a cloak.

— Notice any shift in your body sensations and feelings.

— Who are you without this particular way of identifying yourself?

— What is it like to give it up? What do you gain? What do you lose?

— Notice whether it is easy to let it go or whether it is difficult.

— Is there anything risky about letting it go?

6. After completing these steps for all five identifications, simply be quiet and let yourself experience wordlessly how it feels to be you when you are free of them. Experience your "I AM-ness". . .

7. Meditate on this thought:

"I am the center of my identity. From here I have a sense of permanence and inner balance. From this center I affirm my identity."

Take as long as you like in this step before proceeding to the next.

8. Dealing with each paper/identification, one at a time in the reverse order (*i.e.,* from most closely to least closely identified), pick each one up and imagine it as a cloak that you are putting on again.

— Experience your feelings as you take back this self identification.

— How are you feeling about this particular identity?

— Notice how your feelings and body sensations change as you take back all the identifications, one at a time.

9. Rest quietly for a moment before writing on your *Worksheet*.

Worksheet

1. Who are you without your identifications? How are you different with them?

2. Process each identification with an eye to learning what role it serves in your life and what your resistance is to letting go of each one. Try a question like, "If I let go of _____ then I will _____."

3. What feelings came up for you as you took back each identification?

4. List here any resistance to change which surfaces during this exercise.

5. For each resistance explore other ways of meeting the same needs that do not involve distorting your experience of your body.

6. Comments.

Guiding Words

I hope that this exercise has helped you to identify some of the ways that you are holding on to negative body attitudes and how these attachments serve you. Many women who have done this sequence have felt so wonderful to be relieved of their weighty cloaks that they reacted with anger and refusal when I asked them to put them all back on. I did this for several reasons. Most important, your defensive baggage has a place in your system, and it should be shed *only* when *you* are *ready* to shed it, not just because I instruct you to. Also, this exercise is an exploratory device, not a quick easy way of revamping your whole identity. Our identifications die hard, and the manner and pace at which we shed them is individual and most likely gradual. It is not my purpose to strip you of your identity and leave you naked and vulnerable. It is my purpose to lead you to a place where you can experiment with different possibilities in a safe way.

If you had a strong reaction when I asked you to take back your identifications, that is a good sign that on a very basic level you really don't want them. Yet you are still not quite ready, nor do you have all the tools necessary to let them go. But remember that feeling, remember how much you wanted to be free of all these self-imposed burdens. This memory can help you gain the courage you need to change.

If you had difficulty shedding your identifications or felt relief when you took them back, you should acknowledge the risk in letting go of your excess baggage. For you, the road may be longer. Try to respect your own process and pace.

Francine experienced considerable resistance to letting go of her attachments. She found that her clumsiness was a way of playing the clown so that people laughed with her rather than at her. By seeing herself as unfeminine she was:

> "set apart from women who are physically weak, small and unnoticed, women without stature in the world, women who are defenseless and inconsequential. . . commercialized, vulgarized objects for men. . . . They have been stripped of a woman's power, power that men fear and hate."

And her fat served as an insulation from the world.

> "It protects me from having to be a sexual human being. It allows me to exist outside the normal social order, sometimes as an outcast, sometimes as a privileged person. Sometimes it allows me to be invisible. It protects me from victimization, especially at men's hands. I was raised to be fat. My family only relates to me as a fat person."

In addition she discovered that by identifying herself as unclean she was able to maintain distance between herself and others. The pain of being unlovable was the driving force behind her creativity. Francine is using her body image as protection from sexuality, from victimization, from criticism, from the encroachment of others. She is using her body image as a political statement and a rejection of societal values, and as a way of maintaining her relationship with her family. She is using her body image to increase her sense of her separateness and specialness.

On the other hand, she could learn to maintain her individuality by being more assertive, by learning to say no with her voice instead of her body. She could channel and express her political anger by supporting a cause that challenges society's values. On a more personal level she could explore her sexuality, experiment with new ways of relating to her family, and deepen her awareness of how special she already is as a human being.

If you are not yet ready to contemplate letting go of your excess baggage, it may be that it still serves you in some way. It is up to you to discover how. You may need to do more preparatory work. Spend as much time as you need, repeating the exercises in previous chapters before going on to the next chapter.

It may be helpful for all of you to experiment with your attachments by imagining shedding them in your daily life and watching what comes up for you. By doing this, you can see how the attachment functions. It will also give you practice in letting go of it. It is your ability to move fluidly in and out of states of mind, at will, that is one of your most powerful skills in healing your mind-body relationship.

Seed Questions

1. What are some of the areas of your life where you are using your body image to restrict yourself (*e.g.,* withdrawing from social situations, making yourself invisible, sitting on your power, etc.)?
2. What are some of the ways that you use to imprison yourself (*e.g.,* negative self-talk, selective listening, comparison, etc.)?
3. What would be the benefits of feeling greater freedom in your body?
4. What would be threatening about that freedom?

EXERCISE 14
Woman in a Trap

If you dislike or struggle with your body, you are in prison. You are entrapped by the image you have of your body. You are both the *prisoner* and the *guard*. You are holding yourself prisoner. You have built the prison, your body image, out of many painful memories and negative messages from other people. You have built the prison by comparing yourself to some impossible standard which the media gave you. You have built the prison out of rejection or non-acknowledgment that took the place of needed acceptance for who you are.

Your prison is unique. You keep it strong and impenetrable by feeding yourself constantly messages of negativity and self-criticism, by selective hearing which takes in only what fits your negative self assessment, and by denying yourself the love and acceptance you deserve—*even if you have flaws.* There is no one on earth who doesn't have flaws.

1. Sit comfortably, close your eyes and relax.

2. Go inside and reflect on the very particular ways that you imprison yourself with your feelings about your body. . .

3. Get in touch with how it *feels* to imprison yourself. . .

4. See if you can find an image that symbolizes or really captures the way that you keep yourself imprisoned. Your prison can be a literal one complete with bars, or a more abstract representation. . .

5. Now step inside your image and *experience* the answers to the following questions.

— What is your prison like?. . . What does it look like?. . . What is it made of?. . . How have you built it?

— How do you feel being here?. . .

— Is there a guard?. . . What is the guard like?. . .

— What do you get out of being here?. . . Does it protect you from someone or something?. . .

— What are other people getting from your being in prison?. . . Is your imprisonment protecting someone from you?. . . Whom are you making happy?. . . Whom are you defying?

6. Imagine what lies outside the walls of your prison. . .

7. What are the dangers and costs of being free?. . .

— Consider what you might lose or have to give up (self-pity? sympathy? being a child? what?). . .

— What feels risky? (fear of the unknown and unfamiliar? feeling your power and sexuality?). . .

— What new responsibilities might you have to assume? (learn to say "no"? learn to protect yourself and regulate your boundaries? what?). . .

— What issues might you have to confront about yourself? (stop blaming your body and start confronting what else in you needs to grow and change?). . .

— What is the payoff for keeping yourself imprisoned?. . . What part(s) of yourself enjoy(s) being in this trap?. . .

— Who are you if not this woman in a trap?

8. Get in touch with the you that is in prison. . . Who trapped you?. . . What qualities in you are suppressed by being imprisoned?

9. Let yourself imagine what it might be like to be free of this prison. . . What pleasures would freedom hold for you?. . .

10. Ask yourself: What do I *really* want for myself, to be free, or to be imprisoned? Let yourself sit with the question until your response is clear. . . . If your choice is to remain confined, then stop here and acknowledge your decision. Otherwise move to the next step.

11. Now spend some time fantasizing—just fantasizing, plotting, and planning at this point—how you can escape from your prison. Remember, *you* have created it and *you* know the way out better than anyone else.

Here are some suggestions:

— You can change something about yourself, the prison, or the guard. But do *not* under any circumstances destroy anything. You may *transform* but not destroy elements of your image.

— Ask your prison or guard how you can escape. Then become your prison or guard and respond. The prison or guard is a part of you that represents your negative feelings about your body. Take ownership of this aspect of yourself and the *power* that it contains. As your prison or guard, focus on helping you, the prisoner, to plot an escape.

12. Now *experience* yourself—using all your imaginal senses as vividly as you can—freeing yourself from your prison using all your cleverness. Take as long as you need to escape, and before you leave your prison, take some small momento to remember it by. . .

13. If you have difficulty escaping, come to some temporary conclusion and resolve to try this exercise again.

14. If you have successfully escaped, spend some time alternately looking back at your prison and out at the world. Stay in touch with how you are feeling. . . Are you feeling relief? Joy? Loss? Be open to whatever feelings freedom holds for you.

Worksheet

1. Describe the experience of being in your prison, including how you keep yourself there, the barriers to freedom, and any other details that feel significant.

2. In what way(s) is your prison image an apt representation of how you imprison yourself?

3. What have you learned from this exercise about your reasons for imprisoning yourself and remaining imprisoned?

4. What does your method of escape reveal about the way out of your negative body image trap?

5. Can you apply what you learned to your life (in changes in behavior, development of new skills, shifts in attitude, etc.?)

6. Where do you still feel stuck?

7. Comments.

Guiding Words

Your degree of success or failure in finding and executing an escape from your trap is a good indicator of your degree of readiness to let go of negativity surrounding your body image. Some of you will be able to escape with ease and for you the process of escaping in fantasy and feeling that process will itself be healing. Some of you will get stuck at the stage of executing your escape. In this case, it is very important for you to confront your resistance to being free. Keep asking yourself the questions that the exercise poses until you gain some insight into your blockages. If you were not able to figure out any ways of escape, it is important for you to acknowledge to yourself that you have more work to do.

For all of you I recommend repeating the exercise at least once. It is important to begin to become nimble at finding ways to escape and to give yourself many opportunities to experience the process of escaping. When you repeat the exercise, don't assume that your prison image has to be the same as it was the first time. We imprison ourselves in many ways and there are many images you can explore for insight. Be open to the wealth of your own imagery.

To represent her prison Carla chose a long, rectangular box made of rough, raspy cement that caused pain to the touch on both the inside and the outside. It was designed to keep her in and others out. Her escape involved climbing out, an experience that was difficult and painful. She persisted. To be free meant: "responsibility, adulthood, fear of failure, fear of being too hard on myself, fear of trying and not being 'good enough.' " It also brought a joy in the freedom of movement, self pride, and a willingness to move out in new directions.

In doing this exercise Carla's acknowledgment that *she* was the creator of her own trap was key in her readiness to leave it. Over a period of several weeks of living with this image, she began to find her trap increasingly uncomfortable and uninviting. As this happened, the possibility of true escape became more appealing and worth whatever risk it held for her.

The prison images we choose can be strikingly revealing, occasionally showing us more than we wish to see. Gloria, a woman in her fifties who was in a marriage of thirty years, was shocked and disturbed to find that her prison was her husband's pocket. This represented the crippling dependency that characterized their relationship. Acting and being treated like a child frustrated her. She acted out this conflict on her body, hating it and eating compulsively rather than confronting her husband and the limitations of the marriage. The shock of this recognition propelled her and her husband into psychotherapy. I give this example to show how creative the subconscious mind can be.

Each obstacle is a marker that tells you what work you still need to do. In many cases you will need to make a commitment to do whatever remedial work necessary to clear away the barriers. For some of you the next few exercises may address your needs. For others your work may require further reading, taking courses or workshops to learn needed skills, or in some cases enlisting the aid of a trained therapist who can guide you in further growth.

Exploring and clearing away your resistance to change is one of the most important aspects of *Transforming Body Image*. If you rush through this phase of the work, you will lose out in the end. It is only by clearing away obstacles that the passage along the road becomes possible. So take your time.

X

FINDING YOUR VOICE

*Risk! Risk anything! Care no more for the opinions of
others, for those voices. Do the hardest thing on earth for you.
Act for yourself.*

Katherine Mansfield

We are all overcrowded, cluttered with so many conflicting facets
of our natures that it is sometimes difficult to know who we really
are. Not one of us is so simple and straightforward that we can say
categorically, "This is who I am, and I am the same no matter what
the situation." For example, I tend to be aloof with new people and
very warm with good friends. Which is the real me? Of course they
are both parts of the real me. There are many more seemingly conflicting parts of me: a part of me that needs to be close to nature and
a part of me that wants the stimulation that the city offers; a part of
me that needs solitude and a part of me that loves to be with people.
What is remarkable is that they all manage to coexist.

We all have many subpersonalities that coexist, at times more
peacefully than other times. Each represents a different facet of our
being. Each has a separate voice, together forming a whole. This
whole is not just a jumble of parts, but is cohesive with a center that
has its own voice, wiser and kinder than the rest. In the last chapter
you encountered that central identity—the woman in the trap, the
you under all the cloaks. Your work here will be to get to know this
part of you that has the ability to observe, direct, and harmonize all
the many facets of your being, *at will.* You will also come to identify
the other subpersonalities that figure in your struggle with your
body. When a subpersonality behaves destructively and pulls you off
the course *you* know you want for yourself, it becomes a *saboteur.*
Each of your *saboteurs* is motivated by some positive feeling or intention—albeit twisted in its expression—that is not always apparent.
By identifying your *saboteurs* and learning to recognize their voices
you can pull them out of your subconscious where they can play

tricks on you and thrust them into the daylight where *you* can keep an eye on them. Learning to let go of your *saboteurs* is not the same thing as destroying them. Your task is to identify the positive quality that is trying to manifest itself and to find a positive expression for it.

In this exercise you will meet four of your *saboteurs*. (There are other voices inside you that perhaps you can discover on your own.)

1. Your *protector-saboteur* is the part of you that rationalizes, that argues that maintaining the *status quo* is safer, that venturing out and taking risks is dangerous. It says, "Eat and you'll feel better," "Don't be too beautiful, too sexy, too powerful, too successful or you'll be alone," and so on. Your *protector-saboteur* represents your kind, loving, nurturing qualities, but she/he is killing you with kindness.

2. Your *critic/perfectionist-saboteur* is the controlling, fault finding, never satisfied part of you in whose eyes you will never be good enough, thin enough, pretty enough, etc. It has the ability to analyze, evaluate, and discriminate, but when it judges you and finds you guilty it becomes a *saboteur*.

3. Your *rebel-saboteur* is your fighter who defies the narrow, confining rules of the *critic*. It is an angry, recalcitrant child who says, "I'll show you." It contains your childlike energy, your assertiveness, and your fun-loving spirit. It is trying to preserve your individuality, often fighting for your survival but, unless its actions are channeled constructively, it too is a *saboteur*.

4. Your *victim-saboteur* feels weak and helpless, living with chronic feelings of guilt, defeat, depression, despair, and resignation. It feels sorry for itself, inadequate, scared, and powerless. Its constant cry is, "Poor me, I can't help it." It's the part of you that lets others decide what's right for you. On the positive side, your *victim* is sensitive, vulnerable, humble, attuned to the needs of other people. When it is hooked on pain it becomes a *saboteur*.

EXERCISE 15
Meeting Your Saboteurs

1. Sit comfortably, close your eyes and relax.

2. Find some situation in which you feel self-accepting, comfortable, at home, pleased to be in your body. If you cannot find a real situation, make one up. Let yourself *experience* it fully: the details, your feelings, the expression on your face, the thoughts running through your mind, the sensations in your body, etc. . . .

3. This is the *you* that has chosen to do this work. This is the *you* who has been working hard and sometimes painfully to uncover important psychological material and to make room for change. This is the *you* that is moving toward health. This is the *you* that has a full appreciation and trust of yourself and your body. . . Really *experience* this central, *positive you.* . .

4. See if you can take all the positive feelings inherent in this memory and gather them all together until they flow into your dominant hand (right if right-handed, left if left-handed). Really *feel* the feelings filling up your hand. Now lock all those positive feelings in this hand. . .

5. In the course of this exercise, whenever you want to bring back the *positive you* and the feelings that figure represents, all you have to do is to squeeze this hand. Try it several times until you feel confident that you can do this.

6. Squeeze your hand and bring back the *positive you.* In a moment you will feel a tap on your shoulder. When you do, you will turn around and be face to face with your version of the *protector-saboteur.*

7. Feel the tap and turn around and meet your *protector-saboteur.* Spend some time looking at each other, getting a feel for your particular version of this *saboteur.* Give it a name that describes your sense of how it behaves. . .

8. Using a watch or a timer, give your *saboteur* exactly one minute during which it can do its thing — that special thing it does to you that takes the wind out of your sails and throws you off the course that *you* know you want for yourself. Listen as your *saboteur* speaks and notice carefully any changes in your feelings, body, posture, expression, demeanor, impulses or attitudes as you listen. Take exactly one minute.

9. Did your *saboteur* get to you? Did you buy what she/he was selling? Does your *saboteur* remind you of anyone in your life?

10. Squeeze your hand to let go of any negative feelings you adopted and to reconnect with the *positive you,* that part of you that knows that you are whole and healthy and feel good about the body you have.

11. Now give your *saboteur* exactly one more minute to tell you what she/he is doing for you and what a mess your life would be without this help. Take exactly one minute.

12. Squeeze your hand and return to the *positive you.* . . Now *become* your *saboteur,* really identify with this part of you. . . See if you can get in touch with its attitude toward you. . . See if you can discover the need that drives her/his behavior. . . See if you can connect with the power and energy that this *saboteur* embodies. . . Now return to yourself.

13. Re-establish your control by squeezing your hand, and as you look at your *saboteur,* review what you have experienced. . . See if you can discover the positive intention in your *saboteur's* behavior toward you and the basic good qualities that this part of you embodies.

14. Now verbally acknowledge your gratitude toward this part of you for its good intentions and acknowledge also that you understand what drives its behavior toward you.

15. Ask yourself if it is time to let this *saboteur* go. What would it be like to let it go? What is the payoff for holding on to it?

16. Now it is time to give the *positive you* a voice. Spend whatever time you need to explain to your *saboteur* how you wish to be treated in the future. Offer her/him suggestions about how to be more effective in dealing with you, how to retain the positive while toning down the abrasive, destructive, self-defeating elements of its behavior. (Remember that this *saboteur* represents a part of *you,* so that it is important to find some resolution for healthy coexistence. Destroying this part of you is out of the question and dangerous.)

17. Say thank you and good-bye.

18. Stop here and fill in the *worksheet,* addressing your answers to this *saboteur* before proceeding to the three remaining saboteurs.

Worksheet

Apply questions 1-4 to each *saboteur* separately.

1. Describe your *saboteur*. Include its name, its impact on you, your feelings about it, whom it reminds you of, what it says and does, its style of behaving toward you, what it is trying to accomplish for you, the needs or feelings that motivate its behavior, the power it represents, and anything else that comes up for you.

2. How was it for you to move back and forth between this *saboteur* and the *positive you?* Describe the shift in power.

3. Describe your negotiation and resolution for coexistence. Did this present any difficulties for you?

4. Comments.

●

18. Repeat Steps Nos. 6-16 in turn with the three remaining *saboteurs*.

19. Now gather all your *saboteurs,* and arrange them so that you can see each one and are in physical contact with each one. *Feel* what this is like for you. . . Look at each one in turn and reflect on your feelings about each one.

20. Imagine that a special warm beam of light slowly radiates from the sun, enveloping all of you in its light and warmth. . . *Experience* fully this *feeling* of merging and integrating, becoming one once again.

Worksheet

Some recommendations for further work with your *saboteurs:*

1. When you spot your *saboteurs* at work, talk back from the *positive you.*

2. Engage your *saboteurs* in daily conversations.

3. Write a letter to each *saboteur.*

4. Have each *saboteur* write a letter back to you.

5. Which *saboteurs* feel most central to your drama? Which will be the most difficult to tame?

6. Imagine putting all of your collective minds together to come up with some creative ideas about what the *positive you* can do to quiet the struggle and come to a working arrangement where your body becomes the victor. See if you can join forces toward the common purpose of making you feel whole.

7. Be on the lookout for other *saboteurs* that may be playing a role in your mind-body struggles. Become aware of other trips you are running on yourself, and then see if there is a pattern of behavior. Your new *saboteurs* may be offshoots, or offsplits from the four major ones.

Guiding Words

Finding and recognizing all the voices that live inside of you is extremely important work. They are always in there talking to you. They are like the cartoon devil and angel perched on your shoulder telling you whether to go left or right. Their voices are so familiar by now you may not know they are there. The work of this exercise is to sort out from your interior jumble discrete subpersonalities who are playing important roles in keeping you locked in struggle with your body and perhaps with other aspects of yourself as well. By identifying them, you will be able to spot them at work, to say "Ha! I caught you!" When you can begin to hear yourself talking in this negative, destructive manner, you have the choice of intervening and short-circuiting the pattern by talking back from your center. By understanding what motivates your *saboteur's* behavior, you have the choice to address this need without abrasive self-punishment. Barbara recognized that her *critic* was trying to get her to reach her potential. She was able to take ownership of her desire for excellence and to train her *critic* to acknowledge her positive qualities instead of focusing exclusively on her shortcomings. As she was able to tone down her *critic,* her *rebel* who defiantly overate and procrastinated now had less to rebel against. Listening to her *victim* differently she was able to get in touch with her needs for self-nurturing.

Perhaps you are feeling chopped up by this exercise. That is to be expected. Up until now you were probably not so aware of how crowded you were inside. You have always been this way. Now you have a better idea of who is in there. You may be wondering how you will maintain order, how you will ever feel whole and integrated. This is where the *positive you* comes in. *You* can get to know and understand your *saboteurs* better so that you can harmonize these disparate elements within yourself. The *positive you* knows what you want, what you need, and what is good for you. Right now, your *saboteurs have very big voices whereas the positive you* has a very small, barely audible voice. Your work, beginning now and continuing for many years to come, will be to listen to this fledgling voice. By giving stronger voice to this more central part *you* will begin to take control over your life instead of being buffeted around by this *saboteur* and that.

"But wait," you're thinking, "you said my *saboteurs* are all me." That's right. They represent roles you play, feelings you have, and very often behavior and beliefs you have swallowed whole or internalized from others. They represent more peripheral aspects of *you,* whereas the *positive you* is closer to your true self. Your true self needs a powerful voice if you are to come out whole in this world. Let's face it, the work that you do with this book is only the beginning for most of you. You live in a world that will constantly challenge whatever learning you do here. Visiting your family will be a challenge. Turning on the TV or opening a magazine will be a challenge. But challenge can be a wonderful opportunity, if you have nurtured and developed your true inner voice. It is this voice that can question values, that can talk back and challenge your *saboteurs,* your parents, your peers, the Pepsi Lite commercial on TV. You name it.

Learning to talk to yourself, with your true inner voice, in a way that nourishes you is perhaps the most valuable piece of learning you can do. You talk to yourself all the time — it may as well be good talk. Your *saboteurs* speak harshly to you and your body in ways that make you crumble or rebel. Your new voice is a voice that is full of self-trust, caring, understanding, and compassion. This is the way that you must learn to talk to your body if you ever hope to come to a place of peace within yourself.

Seed Questions

1. Make a list of the areas and parts of your body that you pick on the most. Arrange them according to how severely you treat them.
2. Which areas of your body are the neediest for love and attention?

EXERCISE 16
Body Talk

This exercise is in two parts. Please do them both in one sitting. Please do it with as many areas of your body as you can.

Part 1

1. Sit comfortably, close your eyes and relax.
2. Choose one aspect or area of your body that you victimize most with anger, judgment, neglect, or other negative feeling.
3. Bring that aspect of your body to mind or look directly at it if you can. Become aware of the feelings you generally have about it and the kinds of thoughts you typically think about it.
4. Speak directly to this part of you, expressing your thoughts and feelings without censoring what you say.
5. Now become that part of your body, identify with it, and *experience* how it must feel to be talked to this way. . . Let a response come from this body part back to you. . .

Worksheet

1. What body part did you talk to?
2. What kind of message — content, feeling tone, attitude — is this part of you typically receiving?
3. What did you learn by identifying with your body part? What was its response to you?
4. How often do you talk to your body like this?

Part 2

1. Relax again.
2. Bring your attention to this part of your body and let yourself fully *experience* this part of yourself wordlessly — simply be in communion with it. . . Notice if any images, memories, or associations appear of

their own accord as you stay in touch with this part of your body. . . Notice any feelings that come up for you. . .

3. Ask this part of you if it has anything it wants to ask or tell you. . . Notice your reactions. . .

4. Tell it—with feeling—all that it represents to you, and notice the response you get. . .

5. Ask it: "How do you feel about the way I have been treating you?". . . Notice your reaction to the response and respond to it with feeling. . .

6. Ask it: "How do you need to be loved by me?" and "How can we be friends?"

7. Ask it how it wants you to communicate with it in the future.

8. Ask it what else it needs from you. . . Are you willing to give it?. . . If not, what stops you?. . .

9. Continue the dialogue until you can reach some understanding about how to relate to each other in a way that benefits the whole of you. Take as much time as you need.

Worksheet

1. Which part of you did you deal with?
2. What did you learn about its nature, needs, its reactions to your behavior, the way you can love it, etc. . .?
3. Describe the resolution of your dialogue.
4. Where do you feel stuck?
5. Comments.

Guiding Words

This exercise gives you the opportunity to see more clearly how you treat your body. Some of us deluge our bodies with toxic thoughts. It is important to know what you are doing so you can change it. More important, *Body Talk* lets you experience the effects of your habitual behavior from your body's point of view. What you are doing is opening the channels of positive, constructive communication between you and your body.

Your body is a very sensitive instrument that, if given a voice, can teach you a great deal. First of all it can tell you how it needs to be treated. Later, when you trust it more and have a greater willingness to listen, your body can tell you a lot about its needs, likes, and dislikes. If you will listen, your body will tell you when it is hungry, what it likes to eat, when it has had enough, what kind and how much exercise suit it best, when it is tired, when it is getting sick, when you are under stress, and much more. Your body has a wealth of useful information. But if your communication is a one-way affair, with you dumping negative thoughts on your body, then this valuable information will be lost.

Jeanne talked to her fat stomach who told her how terrible it felt to be stuffed with junk food. It said it wouldn't be fat if Jeanne would stop overeating and start paying attention to her feelings. Her stomach felt unfairly punished and suggested to Jeanne that she could change the situation only by putting the responsibility where it belonged, on herself and not on her stomach.

To create a healthy mind-body communication, you will have to develop a gentler, more compassionate way of talking to your body. It is possible to be kind to your body even if it falls short of your expectations. I used to look at my legs and say all manner of nasty things. Now I look at them and see the same legs, but I choose a different approach. I acknowledge that they will never win any beauty contests. But I see them as large, strong, and functional. They work for me—they are powerful and useful and I am grateful to them. I also see that they could be nicer if I were to lose some weight and do some spot exercises religiously. I see all that. Right now it does not feel important to me but maybe someday I will have a loving, positive reason to make changes in my legs or other aspects of my body. I can then do whatever it takes because the changes will come from a base of self-acceptance, not self-condemnation. My body and I will be working together. On the other hand, if I choose to live with my legs just as they are, that will be fine also, because I know that *I am so much more than a pair of legs! I have* a body but *I am not* a body. I am a person, and I like the person I am. I choose to be kind to me, because that is the kind of treatment I deserve.

I choose to be gentle with my body because I realize that it does a great deal of harm to treat it cruelly and judgmentally. A child who is treated this way will become a behavior problem. Speaking harshly to my legs never resulted in any positive, lasting change. It created a state of divisiveness between me and my body that could only spell trouble. It made me miserable.

Please practice *Body Talk* with all the areas of your body that you malign and carry this practice into your daily relationship with your body. Start to notice when you are speaking harshly to yourself about your body. Catch yourself. When you do, it is an opportunity to put into practice a new way of communicating. As always the choice is yours, whether to continue relating as in the past or to move into new behavior. If you do not feel ready to adopt a policy of kindness and compassion toward your body, ask yourself what it would cost to make this change, what the risk would be in letting this negative practice go. See if you can identify the assumptions that underlie your refusal. Many of us operate on the assumption that if we do not keep harassing ourselves we would go totally to pot. Nothing could be further from the truth. Harassment leads to separation and separation to further battling, It is only through peaceful collaboration that you will make your body-mind a working partnership. Keep working at this until it becomes natural and easy. It is one of the most important gifts you can give yourself.

One way to keep tabs on where you are in relation to your body is to communicate through the "mail." I recommend doing this next exercise periodically during the time that you are working with this book and afterward whenever you wish to touch base with your body.

EXERCISE 17
Express Mail

1. Write a letter to your body.
2. Let your body write a letter back to you.

Guiding Words

Here are some highlights from Carla's letters.

"Dear Body,
I'm sorry. . . you are ruled by a woman who lives in her emotions and head and who takes out her negativism on you. If I'm worried, stressed,

overdoing it, I abuse you, overeat, smoke, don't exercise, don't floss, neglect myself. . . You're such a *good* body—healthy, strong, generally attractive. . . I don't take care of you properly. . . You are my instrument for punishing myself. You serve me so well. I am really learning how much I love you, how important you are to me.

I *make* you unattractive, I inhibit you from being your best. I'm sorry. I really do love and appreciate you. I know I often wish you were different. Really, what I am wishing is that I felt differently about the internal me, not the external you. I'm working on the internal me. Have faith in me that I will learn to love the inside me and quit abusing you. . . . Part of me loves you very much. I'm working on the other part. . . Please bear with me. . .

Always yours,
Carla"

"Dear Carla,

Hi. I know you're going through a rough time right now and I know it's getting better. Really, you get better every year. I know it's hard for you and you take it out on me. I'm strong, I can bear it. We'll make it, sweetie, really we will. We'll be working more together all the time—we already are as you accept your adult female self, your competency, your sexuality, and your vulnerability. You know you hurt me. I don't have to tell you that. But I see you trying and that's what counts. Keep working. We'll pull together! You won't be that silly, perfect ideal you had when you were 16 but I know you know you don't really want to be that. You want to be you, to like you, imperfections and all. Treat me well darlin'—I'll be my best for you. I'm really your best friend. Take care of us—all parts of us.

love,
your body"

These letters clearly reflect the progress that Carla and her body are making in their relationship, the growing affection and the deepening understanding. They both show a willingness to move toward each other for their common good. Carla had no idea that her body felt so positively about her until she received this letter.

Open yourself to your own inner voice and let it help you find your way home.

XI
EXERCISING YOUR BODY-MIND

By this time, if you have been dutiful about doing the exercises in the last ten chapters, you are probably facile in using your imagination. Many of these exercises have required you to be flexible, to move from one imaginal state to another. This next exercise will give you some practice in learning to move from one body image to another, exploring dimensions of size, shape, density, and proportion. Your image of your body is malleable, having gone through many changes in the course of your life, and it can be altered right now at will to become something different. You are not stuck with your current experience of your body. This area is open to conscious choice. Let's play with the possibilities.

EXERCISE 18
One Pill Makes You Larger *

1. Sit comfortably, close your eyes and relax.
2. In your imagination notice that sitting right beside you is a small bottle. You reach over to pick it up and notice that it is full of pills of different colors. The label on the bottle says: "This bottle contains magic pills. Taken as prescribed, you can experience your body in a variety of sizes, shapes, substances, and even ages."
3. Reach into the bottle and take out a pink pill. Put it in your mouth. As it takes effect, you can feel your body growing heavier and heavier. It is as if a series of very heavy blankets were being laid over you, one after another. . . With each one your body grows

---

*Adapted from Robert Masters and Jean Houston, *Mind Games*. New York: Delta, 1978.

pleasantly heavier until you can't even move it. . . You have nothing to do now but to surrender your weight to the earth beneath you. . . Try lifting your arm and feel what a struggle it is to lift something as small as an arm. . . Try lifting other parts of your body. . .

4. With every bit of determination you can muster, reach your heavy arm over to the bottle and take out a green pill. . . Put it in your mouth, swallow it, and wait for it to take effect. . .

5. One by one the imaginary blankets are being lifted, and as each one is lifted you feel your body becoming lighter and lighter. . . Notice the point when you reach your normal weight and then pass it as you become lighter still. . . You are so light now that you are almost weightless. You will notice that your body has become very porous, almost without substance. You feel as if you could almost float. See what it is like to be that light. . . What do you like about this feeling?. . . What do you dislike?. . .

6. But now the pill is wearing off and gradually you feel your normal weight and substance returning. . . How does it feel to get in touch with your normal body once again?

7. Reach into the bottle once again and this time take a blue pill and swallow it. In a moment you will feel yourself growing smaller. . . Now you are four feet tall. . . Now you are three feet. . . Two feet. . . One foot. . . Stop when you reach 6" tall and look around you. . . Experience what it is like to be in the world when you are this small. . . What do you like about it? What do you dislike? But now you are starting to grow again. . . Quickly growing taller and taller. . . Stop when you reach your normal height. How do you feel?

8. Now take a red pill and swallow it. . . You are beginning to grow taller. . . Reaching six feet. . . Seven feet. . . Now you are restricted only by the height of the ceiling. . . Experience being a giant. . . Towering. . . Strong. . . How do you feel being this tall?. . . Take a moment to walk around in this body and experience your body in motion. . . What do you like about it? What do you dislike? Now you are beginning to shrink again. . . Getting smaller and smaller as you approach your normal height. Rest a moment and experience what it is like to return to your normal size. . .

9. Now reach into the bottle and take out a yellow pill. Swallow it. This pill has some very interesting properties that permit you to change whatever you want about your body. Try some of the following variations, noticing any changes in the quality of your movement, your posture and carriage, your feelings about your body, how you feel being in the world, etc. . .

— Large breasts and small hips and buttocks.
— Small breasts and large hips and buttocks.
— Petite and delicate.
— Tall and willowy.
— Muscular and athletic.
— Very thin.
— Very fat.

10. Finally, experiment with your body in any way you wish, changing and distorting any parts you wish. Explore what it would be like to live in your experimental bodies. . .

11. And now come back to your real body. Notice how you are feeling to be back in your own body.

Worksheet

1. Which body image transformations did you find easiest?
2. Which were the most difficult?
3. Recall any observations or discoveries you made while consciously distorting your body image.
4. Describe your experiences with your experiments (No. 10 above).
5. Do you have a sense of how much conscious control you have over your body image?
6. Comments.

Guiding Words

I have asked you to perform these mental gymnastics because they can teach you a great deal. This exercise can give you a sense of how much control you have over your experience of your body. If you can learn to change your body image at will, you introduce the possibility of choosing to live with a body image that is more pleasurable and healthy than the one you now have.

Your body image is not the same as your physical body. Most of the readers of this book have distorted body images that have little or nothing to do with the objective realities of their bodies. Hopefully you will come to a place where your body image is at once more comfortable and more closely aligned with reality. I am suggesting here that you can benefit right now by choosing and adopting a body image that feels comfortable to you. If you feel too short and squat, allow yourself the feeling of more height. If you feel leaden, cultivate the illusion of greater lightness. Since you are able to choose all sorts of pleasant, comfortable states in your body experience, why lock yourself into a body image that causes you pain?

Another skill you can learn from this exercise is fluidity and flexibility. The more readily and easily you can move from one mind state to another, the less stuck you will be in general. This is the kind of mental fluidity that allows negative patterns — mental, physical, or behavioral — to dissolve and change. Greta noted, "my notions of how I really look are shaken. I don't know any more how I look." It is only when we can begin to question some of our precious "knowns" that change becomes possible.

Experimentation and discovery, by increasing the range of possibilities, can also aid in dissolving dysfunctional patterns. As Marie put it:

> "It was fantastic to be able to 'play' with my body image. I could see myself in so *many* different ways, rather than the one negative image that has been implanted in my brain."

There is also important information to be gained by noticing your reactions to certain body experiences. Carol, for example, found that she was uncomfortable at any of the extremes — tiny, giant-like, etc. — because they evoked feelings of separation and alienation. She then had to confront her choice to be drab and ordinary. In general, the transformations that are hardest for you are precisely the ones you most need to do. So please play with this exercise until you are facile in all the shifts.

Finally, it is interesting to note that many, though not all, women have reported that after distorting their body images they returned to their own bodies with a surprising sense of relief and comfort. Many of the experimental bodies they thought desirable, when experienced, brought more difficulties than solutions. Home wasn't so bad after all.

EXERCISE 19
Moving Attitudes

This exercise comes in three parts. Part 1 should be done once. Parts 2 and 3 should be done daily for at least one week. It is best to make both of these sub-exercises a routine part of your day if you want to integrate the changes that you are experiencing into your life.

Part 1: Moving Attitudes

1. Stand up, close your eyes, and go into your body. . . Get in touch with the way you are feeling about it right now. . .
2. What do you imagine you are saying to the world or to any onlooker by the way you are standing?
3. Open your eyes and walk around a bit. . . What does your body say by the way it moves through space?. . . What attitudes are you projecting by the way you move?. . . What are you saying to others through your body language about how you feel about yourself?. . .
4. As you move, see if you can discover where you carry certain feelings in your movement patterns. To do this, take each feeling in turn and think of some situation where you felt this way until the feeling is present for you. See if you can incorporate it into your walk. Then observe how the feeling affects the way you move. As you move through each situation, make a mental note of which body patterns feel particularly familiar, as these are probably feelings that you habitually project with your body language. After each experiment let go of the feeling and walk normally before trying on the next feeling.

   — Any of the identifications you discovered in the *Cloaks of Identity* exercise.
   — Anger
   — Shame
   — Pride
   — Fear
   — Sadness
   — A sense of ugliness
   — A sense of inadequacy
   — Wanting to hide.

6. Once again get in touch with your body as you walk. . . See if you can identify and name the elements in your own body language.

What messages are you carrying around as you move through life?. . .

7. Now I'd like you to try on some new body attitudes as represented by the statements that follow. As you try on each statement, take a moment to let it register. Then translate it in a body posture and begin to walk around as if you believed it about yourself.

— How do you feel moving with this attitude?
— What body language accompanies this attitude?
— What do you like about it?
— What is hard to accept about it?
— What is scary about it?
— How do you imagine others would respond to you?

To clarify your experience, as you let go of each new attitude before trying on the next one, notice the changes in your feelings and your movement as you return to your normal pattern.

Statements

1. "I am perfectly all right just the way I am."
2. "I am a uniquely beautiful woman, inside and out, and I know it."
3. "I am in touch with and proud of my sexuality and my womanliness."
4. "I like myself and feel easy in my body."
5. "I am open to life and to my world."

•

8. Take as much time as you need for this step. Using what you have experienced so far as inspiration, see if you can arrive at a statement of *affirmation* that embodies the qualities and attitude which you would like to have as you move through life, a statement that your body can speak out to the world. Make it a statement of affirmation in the form "I, _____, AM. . . . . . ."

9. Make this into a *moving affirmation,* by moving around while holding your affirmation in mind. . . Let your body explore what it means to be this *you* in terms of body sensations, impulses, feelings, movement patterns, and facial expressions. . .

10. Notice your feelings about yourself. . . Your feelings in relation to your environment. . .

11. Memorize this set of feelings and allow these feelings to flow into your dominant hand (right if right-handed, left if left-handed). . . Lock the feelings in your hand. . . To reconnect with this affirmed body image, all you have to do is to squeeze your hand.

12. While walking around, shift back and forth every thirty seconds or so between your normal way of moving and feeling about yourself and your *moving affirmation.* As you shift, be especially sensitive to the *point* of shift and the differences between the two states (in terms of both body experience and self-image). . .

13. Now sit quietly and, after closing your eyes, imagine that you are asleep. Your alarm clock goes off and you awaken into your *moving affirmation,* your new, affirmed body image. Slowly, step by step, experience your day unfolding. Stay particularly in touch with your feelings, attitudes, your way of relating to other people, and theirs of relating to you. . . Notice the risks you are willing to take or not willing to take. . . What is enjoyable and what is scary about this new way of being in your body?. . . Take as long as you need to complete this process.

Worksheet

1. What are you currently saying to the world with your body?
2. What feelings and attitudes are built in to your postural and movement patterns and where in your body would you locate them (*e.g.,* shame is in my sunken chest and rounded shoulders, hiding is in my downcast eyes, etc.)?
3. What was striking or informative in your reactions to the moving attitude statements?
4. What is your *moving affirmation?.* . . How does it translate into changes in your body, attitudes, and behavior?
5. What barriers, if any, stand between you and adopting your *moving affirmation* as your own?
6. Comments.

Part 2: Mirror Affirmations

1. Every day, first thing in the morning and before bedtime at night, go to your mirror and practice your *affirmation* in the following way:
   —Face your mirror and mentally divide it into a right half and a left half.
   —Stand to the right, and look into your own eyes. With conviction say your *affirmation* to yourself.
   —Now step to the left side of the mirror.
   —Allow your reactions to your *affirmation* to surface and say them to the mirror.
   —Repeat this five times.

2. If you find it too threatening to practice your *affirmation* in the mirror, you can do it in writing until you feel ready to use your mirror. Divide your page in half, left and right. Write out your *affirmation* five times on the left side and your reactions on the right.

3. Keep track of your reactions, since they represent resistance that you will need to work on.

Part 3: Think Beautiful

1. Choose at least one 15-minute block of time each day to move your *affirmation* into your real life.

2. During that 15-minute period (which should be varied from day to day), fix your *affirmation* in your mind as you go through the paces of your daily life.

3. Notice your feelings, resistances, and the reactions of other people.

Guiding Words

Working with affirmations can be a very powerful healing device. Affirmations are antidotes to the toxic messages you feed yourself daily. This is how they work. By repeatedly feeding yourself positive, affirming thoughts, you are building a receptivity to them. Initially it may feel like a rote exercise since you won't believe the truth of your affirmation. With time and practice, belief will come more easily. It is important to speak, write and think your affirmation with feeling and conviction, *even if you do not believe it.* Each time you do, you are sending that message to your subconscious mind. Eventually you will believe it if you persevere.

Don't feel that you have to be married to the affirmation you create in your first go. It may be the perfect affirmation for you at the time—it may be only the first approximation. Be open to letting your affirmation evolve. This kind of work can be very dynamic. It is a form of deep self-exploration that you can safely do on your own.

Here are some guidelines to help the process:

1. Become very sensitive to the feedback you receive when you *think beautiful.* If you are not getting back what you think you want, perhaps you will need to rethink or refine your *moving affirmation.* As an example of this, one woman was walking down the street with "I, Joan, am a beautiful woman" and noticed she was eliciting lewd reactions from men. She discovered two things from this experience. First, her idea of being beautiful had a very seductive component. Second, she really did not want to deal with strong sexual reactions. She went back to the drawing board and experimented with other affirmations until she found one that felt right.

2. The internal reactions or resistances that your affirmation arouses in you can be used to create new affirmations. For example, if some thoughts about your unworthiness keep coming up for you, you can create an affirmation about being worthy, such as "I, Marcia, am worthy of my own appreciation." If you work with the new affirmation a while it will probably clear the way for you to accept your original affirmation, or it will inform you of further work you need to do.

3. When your affirmation becomes too easy, when it arouses no reaction at all, you should consider challenging yourself with another affirmation that can teach you something new about yourself.

4. Here is a rule that should be followed when creating affirmations. Always make it an affirmative statement. For example, "I, Marcia, am a kind and loving person," rather than "I, Marcia, am not mean and hurtful."

Please work with affirmations on a daily basis the same way you brush your teeth. Affirmations are among the best tools you can use for change. I have witnessed profound inner transformations in people who were willing to make this a regular practice in their lives. Are you willing?

Worksheet

1. Keep an ongoing list of barriers and resistance to changing your attitude that you discover doing these exercises.
2. Generate a list of affirmations that you would like to believe about yourself for use in the future.

Other Ways of Moving

Learning to feel at home in your body requires some inner psychological overhauling. It also involves kinesthetic re-education through which you can learn to experience your body differently as a moving, breathing, functioning whole.

In the workshops I lead in the Boston area, I include movement in the form of Awareness Through Movement® exercises, one part of the Feldenkrais Method®. This is a system of movement re-education and body-mind integration that has only recently been introduced in this country. I choose this kind of movement for my workshops because I believe it to be the most powerful and appropriate kind of movement experience for people who wish to feel more at home in their bodies.

The work itself—Awareness Through Movement—consists of slow, gentle movement sequences led by verbal instructions. The sequences present you with situations where you have the opportunity to learn to be *in* your body *with awareness*. There is no one right way to do each movement—you must find out what is right for your body. There is little room for comparison, competition, and self-judgment. You do not imitate a leader. You make your own discoveries guided by your own instincts. It is similar to the learning that a baby experiences as it discovers how its body is put together and functions. It is playful and fresh.

In addition to grounding you in your body, Feldenkrais work can give you the experience of having a body that moves with fluid, graceful ease. This newly found ease of movement coupled with a heightened kinesthetic awareness can lead to a far more accurate sense of your body image.

This work has been very important for me in my struggles with body image. Through it I have gained an enormous respect for the way my body functions. I have also learned to become gentle and playful in exploring my body's potential. Through changes in my body awareness I have been able to improve my posture and correct the movement patterns that had been causing chronic back pain. Most important, through my work with the Feldenkrais Method I have been able to feel that I live *in* my body with lightness, grace, suppleness, and dignity.

I am not including any examples of this method here because it is very important to have the guidance of an instructor who can communicate to you the attitude and tone of the exercises. Although there are only 200 practitioners of the method in the United States, those of you who do not live near a practitioner can experience the method on tape. This is a completely legitimate and adequate way to participate in Awareness Through Movement lessons. In the Appendix I will give directions so that you can find a practitioner nearby. I will also tell you how you can buy cassettes.

Any kind of movement is a way of learning to live in your body, but the Feldenkrais Method, the Alexander Method, Yoga, and T'ai Chi are especially useful because they are all based on moving with awareness. Dance has an expressive and artistic component that can be very helpful for some people and very trying for others. Sports, if you have the aptitude and inclination, can give you a sense of body competency and mastery.

Whatever form you choose, it is important to make a commitment to yourself to find some way of grounding yourself in your body through movement.

XII

LEARNING TO LOVE THE BODY YOU HAVE

We cannot change anything unless we accept it. Condemnation does not liberate, it oppresses.

Carl Gustav Jung

Everything we have done so far in this book is part of the healing process. First we located the psychological wounds. Then we cleaned away whatever emotional debris we could find. Now it is time to apply a soothing, healing balm—acceptance. Acceptance means acknowledging where you are and who you are. It means accepting the fact that the body you have is the body you have. It is not the same as resignation where you despairingly give in and give up. Acceptance will give you the potential to move beyond where you are. It's a paradox. To change something in ourselves we must first accept ourselves as we are.

Please imagine that you are standing on one bank of a stream. On the opposite bank is the change you want for yourself. The best way to reach the other bank is to jump across. The best way to jump is to push off from a firm solid surface, to be firmly grounded on that surface. Let us say that one bank of the stream is the reality of your body, and the opposite bank is the body image you would like to have. If all of your energy is wasted in fighting with yourself and your body and wishing it were different, you will never be grounded and energized enough to move. If you spend your time, energy, and attention in standing outside yourself and judging your present reality or in dreaming of some future time when everything will be all right, you are not being *who* you are or acknowledging *where* you are. And you will never have full access to resources. But if you can accept with compassion the body you *have*—as your home, as the place where you live, as the container for your self, flaws and all, you and your body have the potential to change. By fully being what you are—your magnificence, your power, your vulnerability, your imperfections, your conflicting voices, your struggles — you can become something else if you choose.

The two senses that play the most important roles in forming body images are sight and kinesthesia, the felt sense. They are also the most important in reforming and healing our body images.

EXERCISE 20
Mirror Breathing

This exercise is to be performed at least twice, once in your imagination and again in the flesh using a real mirror. It would be helpful to practice the *Cleansing Breath Relaxation* exercise. It will help you clear away emotional debris that blocks your perceptions.

1. Sit comfortably, close your eyes and relax.
2. Imagine that you are standing in front of a full length, three-way mirror. (If you are doing this in reality, find a mirror in a safe, warm comfortable place where you will be private.)
3. Close your imaginal eyes and slowly undress. . . How are you feeling?. . . Are you comfortable being naked?. . .
4. Take several cleansing breaths. . .
5. Keeping your imaginal eyes closed, remember back to a time in your life when you looked at someone or something that triggered feelings of love, acceptance, or awe. . . Perhaps it was a parent, a child, a lover, a pet, or a beautiful vista, or some manifestation of God. . . Whatever it was, bring it to your mind right now.
6. Let yourself see it now, and *experience* the feelings that such love, acceptance, or awe inspires in you. . . Notice especially the feeling in your eyes. . . Capture the quality of your gaze — the eyes of a lover, soft and open. . . Let the feeling flow into your dominant hand (right if right-handed, left if left-handed). . . Later when you look at yourself and squeeze your hand, you will be looking at yourself through the same eyes of love. When you look at someone or something you truly love, you do not judge or criticize them. You accept them as a beautiful whole, not as a collection of parts or flaws.

7. Please open your imaginal eyes, your loving eyes, walk to the mirror, squeeze your hand, and bathe your body in your gaze. . . Look at yourself as if you were looking at someone you love or at a beautiful sunset or a work of art. . . You *are* looking at someone lovable and beautiful—*uniquely* beautiful. . .

8. Remember if you feel resistance you can squeeze your hand and do the cleansing breath until the feeling of softness returns to your eyes.

9. Starting from the top of your head, work your way down to your toes. As you go, notice those qualities of your body that are beautiful or that you like. And acknowledge each area out loud in words, "I like the curve of my cheek," "I like the grace of my neck," "I like the full, roundness of my belly," etc. Find one part of your body right now and acknowledge it. . .

10. Find another and acknowledge it. Find five to ten more qualities of your body and acknowledge them, remembering to squeeze your hand and do the cleansing breath if you need to.

11. What else do you like about your body?. . . What do you like about the way that it functions, how it serves the purposes of your life?. . . Acknowledge these out loud. . .

12. Find something else lovable. . . Don't forget the side and rear views. . . What else about you is beautiful? Your skin? Your carriage? Your radiance? Your character that shows through in your body? The way every part of you fits together in a whole that is unique to you? The way that you move? Smile? Really *look* at yourself and find as many things about you to acknowledge out loud as you possibly can. Squeeze your hand and do the cleansing breath if you are experiencing difficulty or resistance. . .

13. Have you neglected or overlooked any part of you? If so, acknowledge it now for its own unique quality. . .

14. Once again, look at yourself with tender, loving, self-accepting eyes. And really take in the fullness of your beauty. . . Look at yourself and say, "This is me. This is my body. This is where I live." *Feel* what it is like to be loved with your own eyes. . . See how much of this feeling you are willing to bring back with you after you complete this exercise and open your eyes.

Worksheet

1. How are you feeling in and about your body right now?
2. Describe your experience in the present tense indicating whether it was done in your imagination or in the flesh. Include any feelings or obstacles that came up for you.
3. Describe your own beauty.
4. For each obstacle that came up find some antidote.
   - For every judgment find two positive counterstatements to neutralize it.
   - Take each judgment, chew on it and decide whether to swallow it or spit it out.
   - Create an affirmation to address the obstacle, *e.g.* Obstacle: "My legs are too fat to be beautiful;" Affirmation: "I, _____, can see and acknowledge my own beauty even if I do not fit the ideal."
   - If a *saboteur* is involved, engage it in dialogue and try to overcome it.
5. Comments.

Guiding Words

You were not born out of a rubber mold that came off an assembly line. You are *real, alive,* and *unique.* Your own brand of beauty is unique and has every right to be acknowledged and appreciated — *just as you are.* Through the eyes of love — your love of yourself — acknowledge and appreciate your body and your self. As you practice applying a loving gaze to your reflection in real life, it will become more natural and easier for you. Your body will respond with gratitude for your kindness and openness. The more you learn to love and accept yourself, your body will reflect that love, more and more, and will radiate a greater beauty that will permeate every aspect of your life.

Many of you will find that you have obstacles to deal with before you can fully accept your own love. Please work on these barriers using some of the suggestions in the *Worksheet.*

Toni looked at her real body in the mirror.

"I see myself as a beautiful part of nature, a living being, unique, I see my back and thighs and ass in a new light, my belly too. I have a beautiful body — and I'm able to look at parts using the cleansing breath and see my totality rather than breaking down my body into ugly parts. I feel a sense of oneness with myself, with love for my body and eyes that gaze at myself with awe. I find new power, the power is not threatening right now. I feel peaceful. I noticed my body in a new way today doing this sequence — it's the first time I've seen *my* body — not my mother's and my sister's — or the image of the female family body that I have. I see my own curves, bulges, ins and outs, my own self."

Try not to be discouraged if your initial attempts are not positive. Growing to love yourself and your body usually comes in stages, but there has to be a true willingness to transform negativity into positivity. Contempt and hatred of your body come out of anger. As anger softens, feelings of sadness may emerge about the pain your body has had to endure. This sadness can develop into compassion, a kind and protective attitude toward your body. From compassion can grow a neutral acceptance of your body — neither positive nor negative, just a simple acceptance. Many people stop here but, if you choose, this feeling of acceptance be nurtured into love, not a narcissistic, ego-filled love, but a deeply respectful appreciation for the body you have as an essential part of who you are.

The next exercise presents another opportunity to love your body. When I present it in my workshops I synchronize the instructions with music, Samuel Barber's "Adagio for Strings," which is deeply moving. This is such an important sequence that I recommend you make a tape of it using enough music to fill thirty to forty-five minutes in the background. Pachelbel's "Canon in D" is also appropriate music, or perhaps you have your own musical favorites that are emotionally moving.

Seed Questions

1. Find a person in your life, past or present, whom you fully trust, who cares about you. If you cannot find a real person, fabricate one.
2. Find a time in your life when you experienced love either as the giver or the receiver. It could be the love of a parent, child, animal, a sunset, or god.

3. With your real body, explore and experiment with the ways you enjoy being touched. See if you can differentiate between touches that communicate caring, healing, sensuality, sexuality, indifference, and anything else.

_____EXERCISE 21_____
Imaginal Massage

1. Lie down, close your eyes and relax.

2. Pay attention to your breathing and after taking in several complete breaths imagine that you are breathing in the smell of vanilla. Or if you like you can use a real vanilla bean or vanilla extract.

3. As you breathe in vanilla, _experience_ yourself slipping into a state of deep contentment and satisfaction. Practice this for several minutes until you can do this with ease. Please use this breathing technique at any time during the exercise when you feel yourself resisting or tensing up.

4. Allow your mind to return to a time when you experienced feelings of love either as the giver or the receiver. . . (Begin music) Allow yourself to re-experience that memory as if it were happening to you right now. _See_ what you saw, _hear_ what you heard, _feel_ what you felt. Really be in the image. Let all your senses savor this feeling of love. . .

5. _Experience_ all these feelings of love centering in the area of your heart. . . _Feel_ your heart alive with loving feelings. . .

6. Now become conscious of your hands. . . Become increasingly conscious of your hands. . . Put all your attention in your hands. . .

7. Now take all that loving, all those rich, warm, beautiful feelings of love, and _feel_ them flowing from your heart into your hands. . . _feel_ your hands filling with loving feelings, tingling and pulsating with feelings of love, acceptance, and caring. . .

8. As you breathe, breathe into your hands and _feel_ the loving feelings intensify. . . See if you can keep building the intensity of this feeling with each breath. . . _Feel_ the feelings of warmth intensify as you breathe even more feelings of love into your hands. . . Your hands are tingling now and beginning to glow with an aura of loving

kindness. . . Your hands are incredibly alive and vibrant now. . . *Feel* them. . . *See* them. . .

9. Your hands are now full of love, the embodiment of love. You need only to breathe naturally now to keep them filled with loving energy. They will stay vibrant now even if you shift your attention away from them. . .

10. Now please imagine that you are lying on a massage table or some other comfortable but firm surface. The room is warm and cozy. The lights are soft and low but you can still see around you. You are naked and fully comfortable. You are completely safe. Take the time you need to settle yourself comfortably in this scene. . .

11. In a moment someone whom you care about and fully trust will enter the room. . . This person is in the room now and is walking toward you. . . Look into this person's face and notice the loving, accepting expression. . . This face is full of love and the love is being directed toward you. Allow yourself to drink it in. . .

12. Now bringing your attention back once again to your hands, breathe deeply and, as you do, *feel* the feelings of loving warmth intensify once again. Your hands are vibrant, glowing, pulsating with loving energy. . .

13. Take the hands of your visitor into your own hands. *Feel* the contact. . . And as you both breathe together, *feel* the love move from your hands into their hands. *See* the radiant glow now in their hands as they vibrate and radiate with love. . .

14. Relax now and prepare yourself to surrender. . . *Feel* your body melting into the table as a candle in the sun. There is nothing for you to do but allow yourself to receive a loving, healing touch. . . Remember that you can breathe vanilla to clear the way. . .

15. Your masseur or masseuse is now annointing their hands with warm, fragrant oil. See if you can identify the fragrance. . .

16. Now you feel the warmth of these loving, radiant, caring hands as they slide tenderly along your body, covering every inch of your face and body with oil infused with love. Take some time to fully savor this experience with all your senses — the feeling of warm, slippery hands, the fragrance of the oil, the sound of breathing, the sight of loving eyes and hands that are loving *your* body, just as it is. . .

17. Now your masseur or masseuse is lovingly massaging those parts of your body that you like — those parts of your body that have received positive feelings from you. Feel what this is like for you. . .

18. As these parts of you are being massaged, *feel* some of the positive energy that they hold transferring into the loving, massaging

hands. *See* the hands glow even brighter now. . .

19. Now take as much time as you need to *experience* these loving, healing hands as they tenderly massage and caress those parts of your body that have been the seat of your shame, disappointment, and negativity. These parts of your body are being touched and handled with such love, sensitivity, and caring that they are able to melt into softness and can fully surrender and receive all the love flowing into them right now. . .

20. You can begin to feel your body coming into balance as you soak up love as a sponge does water. . . You are worthy of love. . . You deserve love. . . See how *much* love you can take in right now. . .

21. Look into the eyes of this person who loves you as you allow yourself to surrender to all the love available to you right now. . . Notice the sense of peace in your body and in your being right now. . .

22. As you look at this person you now see that they are beginning to change form. . . *See* their body being replaced by *your* body, and their face with *your* face, and their hands with *your* hands. Breathe. . . There are now two of you, a giver and a receiver. . .

23. As you *feel* your own radiant hand caressing your body and as you look into your own loving eyes, *surrender* to that part of *you* that has the wisdom, and true perception, the love and compassion — the part of *you* that *loves and accepts you just the way you are.* Spend at least ten minutes caressing your own imaginal body with love and healing, being aware of your feelings in response to it. . .

24. See how much of these feelings of love and self-acceptance you are willing to bring back with you when you later open your eyes. But for now spend as much time as you like simply being with yourself and the feelings that you have, whatever they are. . . And then open your eyes.

Worksheet

1. How are you feeling in and about your body right now?
2. Describe your experience in the present tense including any feelings, surprises, or obstacles that came up for you.
3. Were there differences for you in being massaged by another and being massaged by your own hands?
4. Comments.

Guiding Words

Imaginal Massage is usually the single most powerful and healing process in my workshops. It is the sequence that most former workshop members say they practice with on tape long after our association ends.

Here is Carla's experience:

> "I got in touch with the same part of me I discovered when I wrote my letter from my body to me. It feels so warm, loving, safe, tolerant of any mistakes or regrets — loving them and accepting them only for what they are. So warm, safe, loving, happy, pleasant — incredible! Wonderful!"

As for her feelings about her body:

> "A little part of me is still niggling at me — 'You're *not* how you *want* to look' — but that sounds old. I can use that warm, loving, unconditional part of me to answer it back and say — 'I'm O.K., no matter what — all of me.'. . . It's the first time I've ever consciously been able to apply this loving feeling to myself — tolerant of any & every mistake & 'unpleasantness' — I love me. What a base to have!"

The experience does not have to be so dramatic in order to be healing; transformation often happens quite quietly. Sometimes shifts in feelings and behavior can be recognized only in hindsight. Looking back you may say, "Ah, that experience was the turning point for me."

If you found yourself resistant to letting in positive energy, you need to practice this exercise over and over until it becomes second nature to surrender to such feelings. The process of being able to let in good feelings is much like the incoming tide of the ocean. Each new wave expands the ocean's reach onto the shore. Each time you practice a new experience, there is a further erosion of your self-imposed barriers. When you are willing to let down those barriers, you will be ready to heal yourself.

It is a good policy to treat your real body to the healing experiences of massage, lovemaking, or self-touch. Healing can also come by awakening your body to other possibilities: the feeling of a soft breeze on your skin, of your body as it moves to music, the feel of satin or fur against your skin. The possibilities are limitless. Indulging yourself in these ways can help to give you a more positive experience of living in your body. Try it and see.

XIII
PUTTING IT
ALL TOGETHER

In this next exercise you will be moving to a new level of exploration and healing, actively creating your own healing metaphor or myth of transformation. Fables, myths, and tales have long been used to instruct or to change attitudes. A metaphor is a way of expressing a complex idea in a small package (a word or a phrase) and in novel form. It is precisely this novelty that can often shed new light on an old issue. Metaphor frees us from some of the limitations that confront our ordinary waking minds.

Our dreams are one form of spontaneous, metaphorical thinking. Their interpretation can frequently reveal the state of our minds or offer solutions to problems hidden from our waking mind. Talking to the subconscious mind in metaphorical language can be very powerful since the message is frequently allowed to slip in under the radar of our defenses. It is a way of tricking ourselves into healing a wound or solving a problem—in this instance, tricking us into accepting a new body image.

In this next exercise you will be led through a process that will help you create a metaphor to represent coming to terms with your body. This will become clearer as you begin to work through the exercise. To help you further, I will illustrate each step with my own metaphor.

EXERCISE 22
Transformational Body Myth

Finding Your Metaphor

1. The first step is to connect with the *essential* kinesthetic experience of your body, not those feelings that are transitory. Stand up and close your eyes and tune in to your body and *experience* how your body *feels*. . .

2. Write a list of adjectives or phrases that capture your felt experience, and title this list, *"now."*

EXAMPLE:

I came up with an *essential* kinesthetic experience of my body as compressed, stumpy, short, wide, squat, close to the ground, and immobile. Transitory qualities not listed were fatigued and hungry.

3. Stand up again, close your eyes, and go into your body. This time get in touch with how you would *like* to feel in your body. Make a second list of adjectives and phrases that *capture* that experience. Call this list *"future."*

EXAMPLE:

I wanted to feel longer, more upward sweeping, more vertical, flowing, fluid, and mobile.

4. So you now have two lists of important attributes and qualities — one describing how you feel now, and one describing how you want to feel — that you want to make into a metaphor.

NOW	FUTURE
1.	1.
2.	2.
3.	3.
4.	4.

5. Keeping in mind the attributes and qualities of your *now* list ask yourself the following questions to help you find an apt metaphor for this set of qualities. Try to let your answers be as spontaneous as possible. Don't be concerned if you can't find something in every category.

— If these qualities were to be represented by an animal, what kind of animal would it be?

— If these qualities were to be represented by a plant, what kind of plant would it be?

— If these qualities were to be represented by a vehicle, what kind of vehicle would it be?

— If these qualities were to be represented by a kind of food, what would it be?

— If these qualities were to be represented by a raw material of any kind, what would it be?

— If these qualities were to be represented by a building, what would it be?

— If these qualities were to be represented by a landscape, what would it be?

— If these qualities were to be represented by an object, what would it be?

— If these qualities were to be represented by a work of art, what would it be?

— If these qualities were to be represented by a mythological creature, what would it be?

6. If one of these questions suggested an apt metaphor that best captures the essential attributes of your *now* list use that one. Otherwise, let your mind wander freely until you can find any object to represent your body experience. (I found that the image of a tree stump best captured my experience of my body as described in my *now* list.)

7. You hopefully have a starting image or metaphor, Point A. Now you want to find an ending image or metaphor, Point B, capturing the qualities in your *future* list — an object within the same family as your beginning metaphor, *e.g.,* if A is an animal, then B should also be an animal. (I found that a tall, willowy, graceful tree best expressed the attributes — elongation, verticality, fluidity, mobility — that I wished to build into my kinesthetic body experience.)

8. Between these beginning (Point A) and ending points (Point B), there exists a great *middle* that describes a process of transformation that reflects the change that you want in your body. This is where the real work of this exercise comes in.

A --------------------- transformation process --------------------➔ B

Discovering The Transformation Process

You will be working with your metaphors using movement as a way of connecting with the kinesthetic level of the change process.
1. Find a space where you can stand and have plenty of room to move around.
2. Close your eyes, and really *become* your beginning metaphoric object. Completely identify with it. . .
   — How do you feel?
   — What do you look like?
   — Experience your mass, shape, and energy.
   — If you can move, notice how you move.
   — Do you make any sounds?
   — What do you feel like to the touch?
3. Take some time to move around as if you were your object until you get a real feel for it.
4. Now do the same thing with your ending metaphoric object, repeating Steps No. 2 and No. 3.
5. In movement, *experience* the feeling of transforming from your beginning object to your ending object. Move very slowly as in time lapse photography so that you can grasp the essential kinesthetic transformation process at work here. Really *feel* what it means to your body, your movement, and your inner experience to move back and forth between the two images. Try this for several minutes.

Creating Your Myth

Through movement you were able to grasp the kinesthetic level of the transformation process. Now it is time to create a story or myth about how A becomes B, your own unique myth of transformation. There may be many natural ways that your object can transform, as was true for my metaphor. The tree stump was able to send up new growth and to become a tall, graceful tree. You may have to make up a change process. But that is the beauty of myth — anything is possible.

Try not to worry about making it good literature. That is not the point. What you are after is transformation — internal transformation—not Pulitzer prizes. As you work your way through this process, trying one plan after another, you are doing important psychological work. In creating your myth, you are giving your subconscious mind new messages in a form it can accept.

Working With Your Myth

1. Illustrate your myth, drawing what the transformational process looks like including all the characters or objects involved in the process. Perhaps it would look like individual frames in an animated film. Once again, artistry is not the point—use stick figures if you like. The words of your myth will be communicating with the left half of your brain while your pictures will reach the right half. This way you will have a whole-brain experience which is always the best route to learning.

2. Create a *programmed visualization* out of your myth. In your imagination, enact your myth as an unfolding drama of transformation with you starring in the role of your metaphoric objects. *Experience* it with all your imaginal senses. Run this through in the theater of your mind at least once a day for 10-15 minutes for at least one week or longer if you can. As always, the more you work with it the more deeply this can penetrate into your subconscious mind and the more profound your transformation.

Guiding Words

Although many women in my workshops are hesitant as they approach the task of creating their myths, nearly all of them end up having a wonderful time. Even if it does not turn out to be fun for you, it is still a very important piece of the work of *Transforming Body Image*. It is an opportunity to take everything you have learned about your self and your body image, and everything that you know that still needs to change and out of that to write your own transformation story. The myth you create will be, in some profoundly true way, a metaphor for the real transformation you are going through in relation to your body. It is a way of putting it all together. To give you some idea of what is possible, I would like to share with you the myth that one woman wrote. I have so many clever, inspiring, and touching stories that it was not easy to choose only one. I leave you with Antoinette's Story because it says it all.

"Once there was a concrete block who was thick and heavy and clumsy and terribly dowdy. She couldn't wear anything that didn't make her look like a concrete block; very thick through the middle, at the same time tremendously broad through the base. She knew she was a concrete block and disliked the fact and so she wore the same few things all the time and never looked in mirrors. Occasionally she caught glimpses of herself in shop windows and was distressed and depressed.

"It must be understood that she felt she was a block, and always was a block, and would always be so. Yet there were times when she was a gleeful graceful wild strong song of a creature. These times came when she forgot her material being and laughed and enjoyed other people or her lover. But she wanted to feel free moving all the time and to not have her concrete block self rule her. She knew it had reasons for being there, but she battled with it anyway. She was quite tired of this battle for it stole energy needed elsewhere.

"This went on for many years until one day she sat down with herself and said, 'Block, you weigh me down. I'm tired of this struggle. State your purpose and be gone!'

"Of course, the block-self laughed and said, 'I admire your bravado. But you must understand that we are not to be separated as easily as that! In fact, I doubt that we can be separated at all. So we must learn tolerance and live together. I refuse to be painted as the villain. I pulled you through some terrible spots. I came in handy when you ran up against wolf-men. I prevented unwanted comments and whistles that make you so angry you can't think. And being less than perfect physically certainly kept your father from believing he fathered perfectly.'

"She answered, 'Now wait just a minute! I can be all those things without feeling like a ton of concrete! This better-feeling self is due for a coming out and staying out. So let's get used to it. From now on, whenever you feel the need for me to be more human just tap me on the shoulder and whisper in my ear. I'll take care of everything.'

"The block-self smiled. 'It's not that easy! I agree that a compromise is in order, but we have been functioning the other way so long that it will take a plan to turn things around.'

"So the woman stood in her concrete block and concentrated on the kernel of good-feeling inside. The tiny seed was so packed with potential and growth that with the slightest encouragement, it began to sprout, pushing bit by bit up through the cement, around and past each grain of concrete sand, between and over and around each grain, until the first little nubbin of growth gained access to the light and hoisted itself, bringing more sprouts with it. Soon the block was poking out all over with flexible, firm growth. And the sprouts began to grow together. Then, with a little sound, the block cracked and a crevice appeared. The good-feeling rejoiced and redoubled its business, until the block cracked wider. The crack stretched like an earthquake across the expanse of cement. The sprouts took shape in the form of a woman, a smiling woman. She took a deep, deep breath and split the block wide open into many pieces which fell around her. Then stepping lightly over the crumbled cement she twirled and pirouetted into the spaces where the ungraceful block could never take her.

"This scene was repeated many times, for old habits are not easily broken, and each time it was easier and the song-woman gradually gained control of the material self and lived intensely with the advice of her concrete self."

Now it is your turn to tell *your* story.

Section 3
The Road Home

XIV

FOUR WOMEN
IN PROCESS

We like to think that transformation happens overnight. That occasionally happens, although not to the extent that our push-button, miracle-cure-oriented society would have us believe. The profound, inner transformation that leads to self-acceptance does not have a discrete beginning and ending—it is a gradual process of unfolding that can take many years.

I have asked four women who participated in the *Transforming Body Image* workshop at least a year and a half ago to tell their stories. My choice of these women was based on several factors. Most important was the time that had lapsed since completing the workshop so that the process could be seen in perspective. All four women are capable of communicating the richness of their experiences. All of them conscientiously attended the workshop and practiced at home.

Denise

Denise is a nursing supervisor in her mid-forties who completed the workshop nearly two years ago. Denise's body image was an issue for her from very early childhood. Her mother, who had lost her first baby, overfed her other children to keep them healthy. Denise was forced to eat as a child, and by age 10 her weight reached crisis proportions. That was when her father had a nervous breakdown. Before his hospitalization he tried to kill his wife and children. Denise's mother was left alone to support three children with no family to help her.

> "That was my protection, being fat. It created boundaries, it padded my nerves. It gave me a sense of some distance between all of that stuff that was going on and my inner world."

Denise was taken to the hospital and evaluated as obese. Then came the regime of strict diets and thyroid medication. Meals became a nightmare. She longingly watched her tall, thin brother wolf down bread and cookies while she drank her skim milk. Denise was enraged.

She was always plump and large boned, larger than her peers who tormented her for being fat and awkward. There was little comfort from her parents. Her father had always preferred thin women. Her mother struggled with her own weight.

By adolescence Denise became tall and for a time thin. The males in her world began to make sexual overtures. Denise was enraged. She didn't want to be seen as an extension of men's needs, sexual or otherwise.

These conflicting elements in her background were central to Denise's struggles. One part of her wanted to be thin and beautiful, the only way her father and society would accept and value her. The part of her trained to be a person reacted with rage and defiance when she was viewed as an object. Her conflict was played out on her body. Being fat allowed her to be herself.

"I came into the workshop with the dawning awareness that it wasn't just my problem, that I didn't know any women who felt good about their bodies. If they were thin and gorgeous, they hated their ears, or their breasts were too big — there was always something. I knew that I had to begin to get in touch with my body, that I couldn't go on like this, living in my head and living that terrible ambivalence with the diets and the terrible self-hatred. There were three things that happened for me in the workshop.

"I was the only fat one in my group! Everyone else was skinny. I still had this feeling that if only I could be thin that would take care of everything. Here were these thin women who were struggling with exactly the same problem, some of them much worse than me! That was an eye opener.

"I got a sense from you of your own beauty and your own acceptance of who you were as a woman even though you weren't thin. That made me feel that it might be possible for me to come to terms with my own large body.

"The guided imagery was very powerful stuff. I kept coming through to myself as very, very beautiful. And I don't mean in the sense that the world talks about, but more like a. . . wonderful soul. It has helped a lot. It's something that I'm going to have to work with for the rest of my life.

"It used to be that no day would go by when I wouldn't say to myself 'I have to lose weight,' 'I've got to go on a diet,' or 'If only I were as thin as she is.' I don't do that much any more. I'm never going to go on a diet again. Just this spring I gave myself permission to eat and I realized that I have never done that in my life. I had felt guilty about every piece of food I put in my mouth. What I eat now I enjoy. I used to eat in secret, quickly so no one would see me. Now I can appreciate the food and most of the time know when I'm full and need to stop. Sometimes I feel that I could eat the world just to become numb. Sometimes I eat to the point where I can't breathe. . . I don't feel good about it, but I don't whip myself over it. I just start fresh. I refuse to weigh myself. I want to find out who I am from the inside.

"Whatever I do has to come from inside. It cannot be imposed by somebody else's standards. That decision came from the workshop and from my life, too. There was a convergence. That trust and understanding also began to come in the workshop. I can work from that.

"I don't talk to myself a lot about being fat these days. . . part of me loves my big body. And part of me thinks it's wonderful. And I would be very content if I were not in this society, if I didn't pick up all the junk from men and women that I do pick up. There are times when I pick it up and run with it and get into despair and depression and rage. I yell and scream and carry on with my friends. And sometimes I keep quiet and try not to turn my rage in on myself as I used to do.

"I still sense in me this incredible ambivalence, this incredible desire to be thin. And yet now that I am thinner, I know that men are looking at me as an object. On the one hand I'm flattered. But on the other hand I'm enraged."

Toward the end of the workshop Denise ruptured a spinal disc and has spent the last several years learning to deal with chronic pain.

"It's been a time of tremendous growth, actually. It has forced me to try and look at my body, what I've done to it, how I've refused to live in it. It's made me begin to think of taking care of it in a loving and accepting way. . . And I'm trying to become more conscious. . . I'm trying to learn to live in my body.

"I got an idea that it was possible to be free *in my body.* It was in that workshop that I began to have a sense that I could do it. I began to see who I was inside and not focus on whether people were looking at me and what they were thinking. The inner became more important than the outer. My inner life is the most important thing to me in the world and the most astounding. The wonderful imagery work helped me get in touch with my inner life in a new way.

"I keep coming back again and again to those little voices—the *saboteurs*—and tell them to shut up and leave me alone, to get out. I laugh at them and challenge them. There's a new voice in me that doesn't take the *saboteurs* seriously, who's really more in command, 'Let's not be ridiculous!'

"Why does this culture hate women's bodies so much? Why is it necessary for us to be filled with self-hatred? That terrific self-hatred that I've struggled with is not just my own. It is part of every woman around me. That gives me perspective."

Ginny

Ginny, a social worker in her late thirties, came from a family with a history of body image trouble. Her mother, father, and brothers struggled with weight while her two sisters were bulimic. Ginny herself had been a fat child but had begun to normalize her weight as a young adult. Several knee operations kept her from being physically active and left her with a mistrust of her body.

The imagery she tapped early in the workshop shocked her with the level of self-hatred that it revealed.

"I came to the workshop feeling disassociated from and angry with my body. I had expected to do a lot of work on weight and not being pretty and that sort of thing, but it was the real basic stuff — 'I hate my body because it doesn't work for me' — that was incredibly painful.

"When we lay on the floor and measured different parts of the body, I was accurate until I came to my hips. Every single time I thought I was eight inches wider in that area than I really am. I still do that. . . And I still do this exercise to remind myself that my images aren't always in tune with reality, because I still go through some of these trips, but now I know they're trips!

"I got in touch with my parents' past messages to me and I was able to say 'That's them and those are *their* messages, and I'm here, I'm me.'

"The ultimate moment for me was when I wrote my myth, which ended up with an image of me dancing with a woman, circling, and loving and being loved by this woman. This very beautiful woman that I was dancing with (whom I recognized as myself) and I merged. The dance that I danced with myself I mark as a turning point in my life, but I didn't know the ramifications of what had happened for some time. First I felt myself at home and O.K. And I liked who I was. I liked being in my body. That was so different.

"I can literally date from that time a change in my energy, including my sexual energy. I was able to open myself up to loving myself at a very deep level. Something shifted and I loved myself. And most of the time I still do. There are times when I have my spinnings and my distortions, but there just isn't the same level of self separation and rejection that I had before. I don't feel separate any more from my body.

"There have been many profound changes for me. I'm in a relationship, very close to getting married. I'm starting a doctoral program. I got involved with 'Color Me Beautiful' and I really enjoy the vitality and brightness of that way of thinking about color. I've come to enjoy walking just in the last few months, feeling myself move in my body and enjoying it. I feel like I'm O.K., I'm not going to get let down. I've taken some steps to deal with some of my physical stuff like going to a chiropractor. I am certainly aware now. I don't live in my head all the time or from the neck up. I'm feeling vibrant.

"It's an ongoing process. I have the tapes [of the exercises] and sometimes I play one. Sometimes all it takes is stopping and counting to ten and remembering to listen to myself. Let's say I'm walking down the street and I'm feeling fat and ugly and yukky and I've been eating too much. I'm looking in the windows and thinking, 'Ick.' And usually another side will come on and say 'Boy, are you being hard on yourself today.' 'Oh! that's what's going on.' So I stop and listen and do some countering. . . What I usually do is go back to that dance, to my myth when I was dancing with myself.

"I have a new voice that I listen to which has grown stronger. That's what it was about, identifying the old voices and getting the new one to grow in strength and be clearer. The ultimate challenge has been for me to listen to myself and to be open to the messages that I have. It doesn't always work. There are times when I am in periods of great stress when the old voices are most profound. But I find that I at least have a sense that there *is* a new voice. I may not be able to hear it all the time but I at least know it's in there.

"At times I still think I'm too fat. But I've been noticing recently as I look at fashion magazines that I think they're too thin! That's not what I want to be. No way.

"I see it all going back to self-acceptance and to the place where I danced and held myself. My changes weren't all overnight. It was like a little plant that grew. The seeds were strong and they were rooted when I left the workshop and they grew. And I kept on growing. And I expect to continue."

Margie

Margie, a teacher in her late twenties, had struggled on the diet/binge seesaw since puberty. She had spent puberty trying to lose ten to fifteen pounds. She was deeply affected by media images of thin women. Compared to them her body never looked right. She began to feel awkward, ungainly, and inhibited, and she wouldn't buy clothes. Her confusion about her body spread to her emerging sexuality. Feeling disapproval from her parents, her sisters, and her friends, she began to retreat socially. Her experience in the workshop, although healing and illuminating, helped her to acknowledge her need for additional therapy. She tells her story.

"The journal writing in *Transforming Body Image* really forced me to understand my background. I began to learn to accept my body more and to forgive the people who caused me pain. Mirror-Breathing and Chains and Woman in a Trap, especially that one, really helped me a lot because I literally felt that I was in a trap, letting life go by, confining myself to limited choices because I didn't feel O.K. enough to go out and be exposed. I was forced to look at my body and find the things I liked about it, to look into myself and realize that these negative feelings were ingrained but not really necessary. There were things I could like about my body and there were lots of positive feelings way deep inside that had been buried for so long. I loved the exercise where you look in the mirror and at every part of your body and find things that you love. It was so wonderful to me to discover that I could love my body and that was such a revelation, really meaning it. One Pill Makes You Larger gave me the opportunity to feel how it would be to be lighter and heavier. All the different exercises to explore how you feel in your body and the Feldenkrais movements. . . I learned so much about what I could do to myself in negative ways and how I could change that in positive ways. I felt that I had a renewed sense of myself and I felt very comfortable in my body.

"I think that compulsive eating and body image go together. When I eat compulsively it's because I'm unhappy about something. So I eat compulsively, and transfer the negative feelings about myself to my body. Whatever it is that's really bothering me gets numbed out, pushed away, and I focus on the food and on my body.

"I'm more socially oriented these days. . . I had been using my body and my weight as an excuse to isolate myself. It's very rare that I do that now. Because I feel happier and more confident in myself I can project a happier person to other people on my job and relate better and feel that other people accept me. Before I felt that no one would want to relate to me, feeling and looking the way I do.

"I started taking dance classes. I don't think I would have felt O.K. doing that before the workshop. I've also started taking bubble baths and really caring about myself. That's what I learned: that I was O.K. and that I was somebody I should take care of and give to.

"It's a slow process. You might not think that you're making progress at all but then you realize that you're thinking in a different way or you're doing something in a different way than you used to. The things that I learned are going to be helping me slowly and gradually throughout my life."

Francine

Francine is a photographer and art museum curator in her mid-thirties. Throughout school Francine was extremely quiet and so shy that she withdrew from other people. Her struggle with her body began very early. To protect herself she created a split between her body and the inner Francine. The war raged on with recurrent headaches beginning at age three and culminating in adolescence with migraines.

She suffered subtle and not so subtle bodily rejection from her family. Her looks even from infancy were a disappointment to her parents, and the contrast with her older, more beautiful brother made matters even worse. She was the butt of hostile teasing from him and his friends. Her parents never protected her from the abuse—they tacitly supported it. Francine was large boned and stocky. Her mother had weight problems of her own and projected them onto Francine. She took over control of her daughter's body: she chose her clothing, her diet, and sent her to a doctor for diet pills.

"I'm still very definitely in the process of trying to bring my inner realm and my outside together. I just got back from visiting my family whom I haven't seen in about two years. My mother really doesn't affect me anymore. I'm not trying to hide or pretend that I'm not overweight. Since I accept the fact that I am overweight, my mother's perception of me can't hurt.

"I feel much more confident about who I am. The workshop was a good piece of the work. I find that my body image is much more stable. When I'm not dealing with something that's bothering me—when I have some emotions that I'm not really owning up to—usually the first thing that happens to me is that I start feeling *real* ugly and start avoiding looking at myself in the mirror and start feeling like all of a sudden—maybe overnight—I've gotten much huger than the day before. Now I recognize that when I'm under stress I tend to immediately go to my body image and distort it. I've been able to say to myself 'Well what *really* is the problem? You know you didn't gain fifty pounds overnight. What *is* the problem?' That way I can keep things in perspective and not get involved in a distraction. . . and I'm able to relax and find out what's really bothering me. I have definitely developed a different voice—or maybe it was there all along—but I listen to it a lot more. I used to have pretty heated battles within myself. They [the voices] would be yelling at each other. Now my voice is much more compassionate.

"My therapist commented how much more open I was after the workshop. I really wasn't so available for the work of therapy before.

"After the workshop I was a lot more aware of my body and decided that I really wanted to wake my body up so I started seeing a bodywork person—once a month—and we did some emotional work together. It's something that two years ago I wouldn't have considered as being important. I'm still doing it and it's been very good for me. My headaches have decreased. . . I'm living a lot more physically than I did before. I had so much resistance to getting back in my body. I'm still in the process. Just the fact that I'm dealing with a lot of issues like sexuality that I never would have dealt with before is a very significant change. When I was denying my body so much I was not willing to even acknowledge myself as a sexual being. For the first time in my life I feel ready to explore in a non-threatening way what I actually feel. I've been able to acknowledge to myself that I am a bisexual. That has felt very freeing. I don't have to hide anything. I'm still working a lot of this out, but I know now that I'm not so frightened of the thought of becoming vulnerable to another person.

"I am a lot more comfortable with how I dress, experimenting with clothes and with my hair style. With my new job [at an art college] I feel that I can indulge that more flamboyant part of me that likes to dress crazy. I don't feel that I'm too fat to do that. Before I would dress in a funky manner because I couldn't pull off a straight way of dressing. I don't feel that way at all anymore. The way I dress now is a choice, a positive statement. It fits the way I feel inside. I have a confidence that is coming out and is actually showing to other people.

"I feel so much more supported in women's groups, much less vulnerable, less judged physically. I had always felt victimized and angered by the image that society has foisted upon women. I don't feel so controlled by my family or by society. I feel a lot more in control of my own life, and I don't have to be that angry anymore. I have more tolerance for other people and standpoints.

"The other thing that has been important to me is an ongoing support group—formal or informal. I had always pooh-poohed such things—I could make it on my own. I also meditate every day. No matter what is going on in the exterior world, I can go inside and contact my Self. That for me has been a real coping tool.

"Compassion really helps, especially in a stress period. I used to tell myself, 'You're too fat and you can't eat!' That's the worst thing I could do to myself at a time like that—it would send me off on a binge. Now I say to myself 'I'm going to eat something that will make me feel good because I need it.' I don't feel bad about it so I don't put pressure on myself and I don't binge. I'm much more sane about my eating now. Having a weight problem and a distorted body image has been a major portion of my life—my cross to bear. It has affected the way that I deal with the world. It has affected me—now I am able to realize—in positive as well as negative ways. My own struggles have helped me to be a more sensitive and compassionate person, personally and politically. I'm now working to be more compassionate with myself as well."

In their own words these women share the richness of their own transformations. Each one finds herself somewhere along the road homeward—still clearly in process. Their stories are unique, but some themes are shared.

Each woman has come to a place where compassion is the preferred way of dealing with herself, whether through self-talk or through self-caring. At any moment we have the choice to be kind or cruel, to affirm or negate ourselves. Each time we choose the path of compassion we nurture ourselves and grow in self-respect. This inner growth makes it easier to choose to continue being kind to ourselves.

And so on. This shift in attitude, although small in itself, can have a powerful and pervasive effect.

Each woman was able to gain access to her inner being and to experience that core of herself as both beautiful and lovable. This profound self-love is the key to being able to love our bodies, imperfections and all. It opens us to feelings of compassion and permissiveness with ourselves. In some fundamental way it allows us to transcend the identification with our bodies as the reflection of who we are. It allows us to stand back and be a witness to ourselves. Who we are is beautiful. And the body that self inhabits is beautiful by association. Not the other way around.

In going inside, each woman was able to tap the power of her own mind and imagination to heal herself. This realm of mind holds an important key to self-knowledge and self-transformation. Experiencing her inner wealth and the control that she could exert over it gave each woman a feeling of empowerment. It is our own power that can sustain our visions of ourselves as human beings who have bodies.

In transforming herself, each woman was able to sense her needs for further growth — dance lessons, individual therapy, keeping a journal, joining a woman's support group, bodywork, or medical attention. To know what we need we must first be able to know ourselves. To give ourselves what we need we must be willing to love ourselves. This is what coming home to our bodies is all about.

AFTERWORD

No man remains quite what he was when he recognizes himself.
Thomas Mann

I hope that the testimony of these four women will illuminate and inspire your own commitment to making peace with your body. This kind of change takes time. It is a process of chipping away at your assumptions until you reveal the truth that lies buried inside. It is being willing to be yourself rather than the person everyone else wants you to be. It involves learning a kind of unswerving gentleness toward yourself that reflects your desire to heal your wounds through love. It requires a deep commitment to yourself.

Throughout history Woman has been associated with Body and Nature while Man has represented Mind and Technology. Man has soared the spiritual heights while Woman has remained mistress of the dark, mysterious, and powerful realm of the flesh, her body associated with instinct, irrationality, unpredictability, sensuality, uncleanness, evil, the power to give and take life itself. Because Woman has been seen as essential but feared, she has been controlled, as has Body, by being objectified and placed under restraints. This continued objectification of woman's body by society and by ourselves has sustained our disembodiment and disempowerment.

We women today are pioneers breaking new ground and shedding confining roles that no longer suit us. The road is often lonely. In breaking free of the narrow and unnatural standards of our culture we are going against a very powerful historical current.

You have identified many of the voices that express these beliefs in you. You have made at least initial contact with that part of you that is a clear and direct expression of your true self. This part of you also has a voice, at this point perhaps small and faint. This voice will be your greatest ally.

Your challenge is this: To listen to that inner voice that speaks with clarity. To allow that voice to grow in force until it can overwhelm the other voices that compete for your attention. By acknowledging and listening to it, you will be nurturing that part of you that has the wisdom and true vision to know what is right for you. This is not necessarily easy as Ginny, Denise, Margie, and Francine learned, but it is possible.

Our task is to hold on to the vision of how we want our lives to be. The work of this book has been to bring you to a place of greater self-knowledge and self-acceptance. It has also hopefully heightened the clarity of your vision of how you want and deserve to live in your body. By holding this vision above all—and surrounding yourself with others who share your vision—you can surmount whatever obstacles a non-supportive environment throws your way.

You probably know by now that I feel passionately about this subject. I hope that some of that passion has come through in my writing. My zeal comes from a deep place of respect for women—who we are and what we have to offer to the world. It is also fueled by an abhorrence of waste, especially human waste. I have experienced it in my own life, and I have witnessed it in the lives of many other women who have made a career out of agonizing over their bodies.

I wrote this book to give constructive expression to my personal rage about the oppressive standards that I and other western women confront in living out our lives. From a larger perspective, I am both frightened and saddened as I watch today's women trying to conform to these standards at the expense of much of their human potential. This is a tragic waste, and it is my passionate belief that something must be done about this on a cultural and ideological level. It is my hope that this book will serve not only as a vehicle for self-improvement but as a way of sensitizing women to the need for change on a much larger scale.

When enough people change their consciousness to embrace a new set of values, the values of their culture change. We have all witnessed this in the major societal changes set in motion by the Women's Movement. When I lead my workshops or teach classes in body image I feel like a small voice in the wilderness. I can touch relatively few women at a time. Their changes cause a tiny ripple that is easily overwhelmed by the cultural currents they confront in their lives. A book can reach a larger audience. It is my hope that you will come away from reading this book with greater enlightenment than you had before, with a more profound and respectful sense of who you are as a person. Then those of you who have been touched by this process will in turn touch and support others until the ripple becomes a wave and finally a tide that cannot be ignored.

Many women — and therapists — fail to take the subject of woman's body image seriously, seeing it as a superficial concern. For many, this lack of concern comes from ignorance of the facts. While our outer appearances may indeed be superficial when compared to the depth of our inner beings, there is nothing shallow about the pain of separation between a woman and her body, nothing light about the waste of lives spent in trying to be something other than what we are.

Isn't it about time we all learned to love the bodies we have?

RESOURCES

Books Related to Body Image

Bennett, W. & Gurin, J. *The Dieter's Dilemma: Eating Less and Weighing More.* New York: Basic Books, 1982.

Brownmiller, S. *Femininity.* New York: Simon and Schuster, 1984.

Chernin, K. *The Obsession: Reflections on the Tyranny of Slenderness.* New York: Harper & Row, 1981.

Lichtendorf, S.S. *Eve's journey: The Physical Experience of Being Female.* New York: Berkley Books, 1983.

Millman, M. *Such a Pretty Face.* New York: W.W. Norton, 1980.

Orback, S. *Fat Is a Feminist Issue, II.* New York: Berkley Books, 1982.

Roth, G. *Feeding the Hungry Heart.* New York: New American Library, 1983.

Cassette Tapes

Transforming Body Image: Learning to Love The Body You Have. Set of seven 90-minute tapes. A catalog is available from Body-Mind Tapes, 88 West Goulding Street, Sherborn, MA 01770.

The Feldenkrais Method®: Awareness Through Movement®.

Books:

Feldenkrais, M. *Awareness through movement: health exercises for personal growth.* New York: Harper & Row, 1977.

Feldenkrais, M. *The elusive obvious.* Cupertino, CA.: Meta Publications, 1981.

Mind-Body Tapes:

For catalog write Mind-Body Tapes, 88 West Goulding Street, Sherborn, MA 01770.

Practitioner Directory and Brochure:

Write to The Feldenkrais Guild, P.O. Box 11145, San Francisco, CA 94101

Notes

Notes

Notes

Notes

Notes

Notes

Notes

Notes

Notes